REAL KIDS, REAL FAITH

REAL KIDS, REAL FAITH

Practices for Nurturing Children's Spiritual Lives

Karen Marie Yust

Foreword by
Eugene C. Roehlkepartain

JOSSEY-BASS
A Wiley Imprint
www.josseybass.com

Published by Jossey-Bass
A Wiley Imprint
989 Market Street, San Francisco, CA 94103-1741   www.josseybass.com

Jossey-Bass books and products are available through most bookstores. To contact Jossey-Bass directly call our Customer Care Department within the U.S. at 800-956-7739, outside the U.S. at 317-572-3986, or fax 317-572-4002.

Jossey-Bass also publishes its books in a variety of electronic formats. Some content that appears in print may not be available in electronic books.

Library of Congress Cataloging-in-Publication Data
Yust, Karen-Marie.
Real kids, real faith: practices for nurturing children's spiritual
lives / Karen Marie Yust; foreword by Eugene C. Roehlkepartain.
p. cm.—(The families and faith series)
Includes bibliographical references and index.
ISBN 0–7879–6407–7 (alk. paper)
1. Christian education of children. 2. Children—Religious life. 3.
Spiritual life—Christianity. I. Title. II. Series.
BV1475.3.Y87 2004
268'.432—dc22
2003025937

Printed in the United States of America

FIRST EDITION

HB PRINTING   10 9 8 7 6 5 4 3 2 1

THE FAMILIES AND FAITH SERIES

The Families and Faith Series is devoted to exploring the relationship between the spiritual life and our closest human relationships. From one generation to the next, faith and families are deeply intertwined in powerful ways. Faith puts all of life, including family life, in such a large perspective that it invites the gratitude, wonder, and hope so badly needed in the middle of the complexities and struggles of existence. On the other hand, faith becomes real only as it lives through concrete human relationships. Religion needs families and communities where the generations gather together and share and celebrate what it means to love God and to love others. At their best, faith and families are immersed in grace, and this series hopes to be a resource for those seeking to make love real in their families, congregations, and communities.

Diana R. Garland
> Director, Baylor Center for Family and Community Ministries
> Baylor University

J. Bradley Wigger
> Director, Center for Congregations and Family Ministries
> Louisville Presbyterian Theological Seminary

SERIES EDITORS

TITLES IN THE FAMILIES AND FAITH SERIES
Sacred Stories of Ordinary Families: Living the Faith in Daily Life
> Diana R. Garland
Let the Children Come: Reimagining Childhood from a Christian Perspective
> Bonnie J. Miller-McLemore
The Power of God at Home: Nurturing Our Children in Love and Grace
> J. Bradley Wigger
Seasons of a Family's Life: Cultivating the Contemplative Spirit at Home
> Wendy M. Wright
Real Kids, Real Faith: Practices for Nurturing Children's Spiritual Lives
> Karen Marie Yust

With gratitude to David, Paula, and Michael
for all they have taught their mother

CONTENTS

✧

FOREWORD

Conventional wisdom tells us that young adults who dropped out of active religious involvement in their teens or twenties start reconnecting to church, synagogue, mosque, or temple when they have children. Whether out of a genuine spiritual quest or a belief that it's just something they are supposed to do, parents somehow want their children to be grounded in faith and a faith tradition.

But parents are not always sure what they want for their child or what their children need in order to get it. And, too often, they do not have positive memories from their own childhood to guide them. They may recount a strict, rigid approach that insisted that they say (or *not* say), do (or *not* do), and think (or *not* think) certain things. Or they may recall a nonchalant indifference based on the assumption that "kids need to figure this stuff out for themselves." Neither approach seems adequate or appropriate.

When young adults become parents, they either revert to what their parents did or do just the opposite, thinking anything would be better than that. Chances are, neither group of parents is happy with the default approach. They want to pass their faith on to their children, but they do not really know other options.

There is another way, an approach to spirituality" with young children that celebrates children's gifts of faith and the spirit that dwells within them while also recognizing the important ways that parents and other adults nurture that spirit through thoughtful, formative practices—intentional ways of living—that shape their children's lives and faith.

This approach is embodied in this groundbreaking, one-of-a-kind book. *Real Kids, Real Faith* is both thoughtful and practical, affirming and challenging, steeped in traditions, and grounded in contemporary life. By avoiding pat answers on the one hand and abstract philosophy on the other, Karen Marie Yust offers the inspiration and tools needed to nurture life-shaping faithfulness in children.

Karen Marie Yust's approach builds on—and contributes significantly to—the burgeoning field of study of spirituality in children. Scholars are starting to recognize that the "cute" things children say about life and God may not match adults' sophisticated belief systems, but they do grow out of the genuine and important processes of making sense of the world and their place in it. Yes, children can be crabby and demanding and possessive. But they can also be remarkably generous, caring, and compassionate. While adults too quickly become skeptical and cynical, children revel in miracle and mystery. More and more, experts and parents alike are recognizing that children teach us, just as we seek to teach them.

Be careful, then, when you embark on this journey of nurturing children's spiritual lives. You may have gotten into this because you want something more for your children. But, inevitably, the approach offered in this book points toward a journey you take together with your children. Nurturing spirituality is not something you do to or for your children; it is something you do with your children. And with your children, you will learn, discover, and grow in ways that you cannot predict or control. It will change you.

And you will all be better for it.

Eugene C. Roehlkepartain
Director, Family and Congregation Initiatives
Search Institute

PREFACE

I love, admire, and respect children. The three whom I have the privilege of parenting constantly amaze me with their creativity and their openness to new ideas and experiences. They also demand tremendous energy with their questions, their not-so-occasional bickering, and their persistent experimentation. I want to be a "good" parent, and sometimes I am not sure just what good parenting ought to look like in a particular moment. But in the face of my children's remarkable willingness to keep working with me and their resilience when I get it wrong, I've come to believe that being a good parent is as much a matter of desire and persistence as it is getting it right at any given time. It's about the very things that I appreciate in my children: tackling challenges with creativity and remaining open to what the next moment or day brings. It's also about the more difficult parts: questioning what one has done and will do next; "debating" (because, of course, adults *never* bicker) with one's spouse, extended family, and friends the merits of various family rules, practices, and traditions, and trying out various approaches to see if they help us accomplish the work of caring for our children in ways that fulfill our parenting goals. As I experience it, all this work has to be done with a sense of appreciation for who our children are today and who they may become in the future. That is no easy task.

I've written this book, not because I always succeed at being a good parent but because I am (like you, I suspect) committed to becoming an ever-better parent. If we lived in the same neighborhood, we might meet on the occasional Saturday morning at the local coffee shop to chat and compare notes about our strategies and experiences. We might hang out in our front yards together while our children ride their bikes up and down the street. We might even call one another up after a particularly rough day and consult about the difficulties we're encountering with one child or another.

However, we live many miles apart; we've likely never even met, and so the stories about parenting in these pages are mostly my own. As you read them, I hope they will bring to mind your own experiences. I also hope you'll remember that behind every story about "getting it right" are many less stellar attempts to guide my children well. My household is far from perfect, and my children are quite capable of listing my numerous parenting blunders and faults. I've even shared a few of them along the way to "keep it real," as my teenager would say. I hope both kinds of stories help you do the same.

ACKNOWLEDGMENTS

Books are shared labors, even when written by a single author. By their willingness to take time from their own projects to read and comment on this manuscript, Ron Anderson, Chris Coble, and Cathie Kelsey challenged me to clarify, expand, and refine various ideas so that my conversation with the reader might be more interesting and flow more smoothly. I am grateful for their counsel regarding how to balance the inclusion of scholarship and personal experience in a book that doesn't permit neat distinctions among my roles as mother, minister, and scholar. I especially thank Ron for his careful attention to the discussions of theological themes, prayer, and congregational life; Chris for the stories of his own family's experiences and his historical references; and Cathie for her theological acumen and for enlisting her husband, Terry Tice, in a marathon read-aloud session designed to check whether my writing style was reader-friendly. I greatly appreciate their spirit of collegiality and collaboration.

Others have also contributed to the shape of this volume. Before her death, Sarah Polster of Jossey-Bass sat in my office and shared her dream of a book series on spirituality and families, and I am delighted that Sheryl Fullerton and Julianna Gustafson caught her vision and are carrying it forward. Julianna and her publication team have been a pleasure to work with; I thank them for their attentiveness and responsiveness through the entire writing and publication process. Diana Garland and Brad Wigger, coeditors of the *Faith and Families* series, have provided strong support through their writer conferences and comments; it is an honor to be part of their project.

Some of the observations and reflections included in these pages are the result of research conducted as part of the Faith Formation in Children's Ministries Project, a three-and-a-half-year exploration of how children's spirituality is understood and nurtured in mainstream Protestant congregations in the United States. Funding for this project was provided by the Lilly Endowment, Inc., and Chris Coble provided support and encouragement for the work in his role as the program officer for the grant. Although my findings are often represented more implicitly than explicitly in this particular text, the opportunity to focus sustained attention on the topic of children and spirituality was essential to the writing of the book. I am also grateful to the several congregations and numerous parents who agreed to talk with me and let me observe their children.

Other ideas and observations stem from the many workshops on children, spirituality, and religious traditions that I have conducted for parenting groups and churches over the last dozen years. The idea for such workshops originated with Cyndie White of the Harvard University Office for Work and Family, who dared to have me speak on campus four times as part of her programming for graduate students, faculty, staff, and the neighboring community. She more than anyone else has seen the evolution of my ideas over time, and the parents with whom she and other workshop organizers brought me into contact taught me much about the questions and concerns of contemporary families around this topic.

I thank my colleagues at Christian Theological Seminary for reading and discussing with me the introduction and first chapter of the manuscript during our monthly faculty colloquium and for granting me a semester's sabbatical leave during which I could finish my writing. I appreciate the opportunity to discuss many of these ideas with students, both in class and more informally in the halls. It is indeed a gift to reside in a community of teaching and learning.

My husband, Brady, and my children, David, Paula, and Michael, deserve my deepest thanks, for they not only continue to live the reality of this book with me but they have endured the trials of the writing process with (usually) patience and good humor. For their willingness to endure leftovers or take-out pizza on the nights I stayed in the office late writing, their permission (so long as I didn't embarrass them) to tell stories about their lives, and their good-natured teasing when I got on my soapbox, I am in their debt. My thanks, too, to

Oskar and Olivia Iobst for serving as frequent reminders of what life is about for an infant and two-year-old, and to their parents, Erin and Matthew, for sharing their children with me so generously. There is nothing like a hug from a child, whether one's own or "borrowed," to keep one motivated while writing a book on children and spirituality! Thank you all.

INTRODUCTION

The Quest to Support Our Children's Spiritual Lives

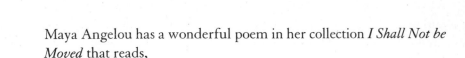

Maya Angelou has a wonderful poem in her collection *I Shall Not be Moved* that reads,

> Midwives and winding sheets
> know birthing is hard
> and dying is mean,
> and living's a trial in between.
> Why do we journey, muttering
> like rumors among the stars?
> Is a dimension lost?
> Is it love?

The sentiment expressed and questions posed by this poem characterize the perspectives and musings of many of us. We are afraid that our contemporary culture has lost touch with love and compassion. In varied ways, we are wondering, what is the nature of life in our time and place? Have we lost touch with what might nurture and sustain us in our living? What might that sustaining force be? How do we connect with this force? These are spiritual questions that shape our adult lives because we do not want to be wandering through the trials of life without a sense of belonging and purpose. And for those of us who live and work with children, these are questions we ask on behalf of our children, hoping to spare them some of our own doubts and misgivings about life and its meaning. Thus we set out on a journey in search of meaning for ourselves and the children we love, looking around us for resources and provisions to guide and sustain us on our way.

A SEARCH FOR RESOURCES TO GUIDE US

Finding resources can be more difficult than we first imagine. Our culture professes to love children, and our businesses market numerous products to parents and children that they claim are necessary for a "good" childhood. We have "Happy Meals" and *Big Comfy Couch;* we have digital cameras for recording each developmental milestone and video devices for spying on the babysitter. We can buy classic children's books like *The Cat in the Hat; Little Women; Robinson Crusoe;* and *Good Night, Moon,* and put them on our children's shelves alongside contemporary favorites like Tomie de Paola's *Strega Nona* and the *Harry Potter* books. Disney videos abound for our children's entertainment; they've been joined by *Veggie Tales* and the film industry's myriad "family entertainment" flicks. But few of these products help us or our children explore the bigger questions in life. We know that the happiness promised in a Happy Meal is fleeting, that we can't remain sequestered in comfortable places, that images captured electronically don't tell the whole story, that books don't explain everything we want to know about our lives, and that movies provide more of an escape from reality than a full engagement with the problems we encounter. Our children experience heartache, frustration, and confusion as well. Both we and they need something more in our lives than the stuff and the fantasies that companies want to sell us. We want to find a more nurturing and dependable source of purpose and meaning. And then we want to establish a connection with this source that will endure throughout our lives and the lives of our children.

Sometimes we suspect that our children are more attuned to

such a source than we are ourselves. We applaud their innocence and purity and wish that we could regain their rather charming naïveté. At other times, we deplore their childishness, wondering what monster has taken over our child's body as we attempt to cope with tantrums, biting, stubborn defiance, and other commonplace childhood events. Life today is such that we want our children to be both innocent and sophisticated, both compassionate and competitive. We know that society judges children primarily by their cognitive abilities. We agree, at least in part, with society's intense focus on containing and channeling children's energies and interests into a productive adult life. We tend to assume, because it is what we've been taught, that childhood today is a training period for "real" life and that children's development is the most important purpose of parenting and teaching children. But training for some future life as an adult is not necessarily the primary purpose of childhood, although it is a very real aspect of children's lives.

If we ask ourselves whether we've lost touch with something that might nurture and sustain human lives, we have an opportunity to shift our thinking away from developmental models of adult-child interactions to models of nurture and sustenance that value both the moment and children as they are in the moment. We can imagine creating places and ways for children to encounter that which sustains their living, however we might define it. We can embark on a spiritual journey with children, both teaching them and learning from them along the way.

Anne Lamott has a chapter in her book *Traveling Mercies* titled, "Why I Make Sam Go to Church." Sam is Lamott's son, and he is less than enthusiastic about churchgoing. But Lamott writes that she still requires him to go because

> I want to give him what I found in the world, which is to say, a path and a little light to see by. Most of the people I know who have what I want—which is to say, purpose, heart, balance, gratitude, joy—are people with a deep sense of spirituality. They are people in community, who pray, or practice their faith; they are Buddhists, Jews,

Christians—people banding together to work on themselves and for human rights. They follow a brighter light than the glimmer of their own candle; they are part of something beautiful.

Anne Lamott makes a point that I think is crucial to our understanding of children and spirituality. Our spiritual lives are something we discover and explore as part of a community of faithful people seeking to act in ways consistent with their values. This community can be as small as a household or as large as the major religious traditions of the world. But whatever its size, it is essential to our children's spiritual formation and their acquisition of a language and rituals that help them to identify and express their values and beliefs.

For over a decade, I have been talking with parents and other adults about what they hope for children and children's spirituality. As I've listened to participants in my research projects, parenting workshops, and congregations, these are some of the dreams I've heard expressed:

"Maybe the most important thing [for children] is acceptance for who you are."

Children need something "to fall back on" in difficult times.

"I want my kids to get positive role models and positive influences from other 'good' kids. I want them to learn [in church] the things they don't get in school: how to be a good person, a caring person, and to treat others with respect—to learn to discern who are good kids to play with and who to avoid."

Children need "experience in leadership."

Give children "a good place to hang out"—one that is safe and free of negative influences.

Adults need to provide "a broad sense of religion."

Children should have a "tremendous sense of community" that provides a "feeling of extended family."

Children need socialization in "basic principles," for example, fairness, acceptance, equal opportunity.

These are good dreams for children. They point to the fact that one of the primary reasons parents bring their children to churches and synagogues is that we hope the connection with a faith community will provide something that is missing from other arenas of childhood. Whether we name this missing part "morals" or "safety" or "acceptance," we are seeking something that will take our children beyond the confines of culture into a more spiritual realm where love, compassion, and peace hold greater sway than hate, disregard, and violence.

I want to challenge us, however, to dream bigger dreams than these—to dream that

- Our children will not only discover a safe place to belong but a community that challenges them to discern their purpose and vocation in life as children of God.
- Our children will learn how to resist those aspects of our American culture that have already disappointed us with their empty promises and stress-inducing side effects.
- We, alongside our children, might work together toward understanding how we are to live our lives as spiritual beings.

Some developmental "experts" argue that children who are younger than twelve years old are too young to engage in the spiritual life in any meaningful way. These folks encourage parents and religious educators to focus on promoting trust relationships, building self-esteem, and laying foundations for later beliefs. For them, the primary goal of children's spiritual formation is keeping children entertained with religious activities until they are old enough to engage in real religious practices. They tend to define "true spirituality" as adhering to a particular set of beliefs and values or a specific way of making decisions. Wonder, experiential interpretations, and intuitively grasped insights into the mystery of God are then given little value, compared to a proper religious understanding of the meaning of life.

Although I do not want to dismiss the value of religious understanding as one aspect of spirituality, I think this perspective fails to take account of the full nature of the spiritual life. To seek after and be sought by God is a lifelong process of being in relationship with a mystery much bigger than our minds can grasp, even with the maturity of adulthood. We can never stop asking—or encouraging our children to ask—where and how we might share in the loving relationship that we, and God, long for.

Over twenty-five years ago, religious educator John Westerhoff posed a question that captured the concern of many people. He asked, in a book by the same title, "Will our children have faith?" His answer, put succinctly, was that children will have faith if the adults in their lives accompany them on their spiritual journey, providing children with opportunities to experience the life of faith at home and in the religious community. Westerhoff's book was reissued in the year 2000, in part because his question continues to be a concern of parents and religious communities. We want our children's lives to be meaningful, and we are afraid there is not much in the twenty-first century that a child can have faith in. We may have lost faith ourselves and not know where to find it again. Thus it is time for us to risk embarking on a spiritual quest with our children, seeking faithfulness together.

CONTENTS OF THIS BOOK

The following chapters serve as guides for this spiritual quest. Chapter One suggests that we begin our quest with an exploration of the concept of faith: what it is, what it isn't, and how even very young children have it. This chapter also suggests that we cannot talk about faith without considering six other concepts dear to the hearts of most parents and adults who work with children: belonging, giftedness, thanksgiving, hospitality, understanding, and hope. We will look at the ways in which children's physical, cognitive, emotional, and social development affect their expressions of faith and their spiritual awareness. By focusing on the *capabilities* of children at various ages, we will discover how we can better nurture and support their spiritual formation.

Chapter Two focuses on how we can create a spiritual world for children to inhabit at home and in the religious community. With the omnipresence of images like Big Bird, Mickey Mouse, and Winnie-the-Pooh in our general culture, we are well aware of the power that imaginary commercial worlds can have for children. This chapter explores ways in which we can intentionally create a religious culture for children that is peopled with religious characters, religious symbols, and religious language so that they incorporate the religious into their lives as normal and desirable. It suggests ways in which parents and religious educators can help children inhabit the two worlds of American culture and religious culture simultaneously, much as immigrant families have learned to do in order to preserve their ethnic culture in a new land.

Chapter Three guides us into the art of religious storytelling. We begin to explore ways in which we can help children hear and speak aloud the faith story and their own stories so that these narratives become intertwined in children's lives. This chapter also includes a discussion of different types of storytelling and storybooks, suggesting ways each type might contribute to spiritual formation.

Chapter Four is a guide to the adventure of learning a second language, that is, the language of the religious tradition with which one has chosen to affiliate. The process of becoming fluent in the language of spirituality is similar to the process one follows for learning any language. This chapter helps make the connections between general theories of language acquisition and literacy and the delightful task of learning to speak, "read," and understand the language of the religious life. Its goal is to guide us into spiritual bilingualism.

Having dwelt for two chapters in the good company of words and stories, we move to Chapter Five, which invites us to explore the value of silence and stillness for our own and our children's spiritual formation. Conventional wisdom claims that children cannot sit still or focus their attention for more than a few minutes, but children are capable of more than we typically give them credit for. This chapter distinguishes between the cultural admonishment that children be quiet and the purposeful use of silence as a way to listen to God. It explores the ancient art of lament as a means of connecting children's daily experiences with the promises of God and provides information about cultivating a variety of prayer forms.

Also contrary to popular belief is the notion that children can encounter abstract ideas about God, faith, and religious experience and order them in positive ways that meet their current spiritual needs. Chapter Six explores how children make sense of common religious concepts. It encourages the adoption of a spiritually formative process of asking questions and receiving answers in order to promote a thoughtful religious curiosity in children. It also offers examples of how children's theological interpretations of central religious stories and of the world change as they develop.

Chapter Seven challenges the assumption that children's faithfulness should be equated with well-mannered obedience to parents and other adults. It explores the many ways in which children are capable of reaching out to others with compassion and service. It provides ideas for nurturing children's respect and care for others and suggests ways we can support children in the development of a dynamic spiritual life characterized by a balanced movement between inward reflection and outward service.

The concluding chapter celebrates the ways in which experiences of religious community can powerfully shape children's lives and the lives of adults as well. It portrays faith communities as partners in the parental quest to nurture children's spiritual lives and suggests characteristics that parents should look for in a congregation when they decide to join a religious community. It advocates the intentional inclusion of children in the life of the faith community and urges familial commitment to full participation in the congregation of their choice.

Throughout the book are stories and examples taken from my own experience as a parent, as well as my work with children, parents, and religious educators as a community speaker and parish pastor for eleven years; my extensive research with congregational children's ministries is also reflected. These stories and examples are meant to be signposts along the way of our spiritual quest. They tell us something about where children dwell in the spiritual landscape, remind us of how others have traveled the road before us, and point us toward new horizons of thinking. They remind us that nurturing children's spiritual lives is not a theoretical discussion but an aspect of our very concrete lives as parents and educators of children. And they allow us to be taught by the voices and actions of the very ones whose young lives have motivated us to read (and write) this book.

REAL KIDS,
REAL FAITH

Chapter 1

WHAT'S FAITH GOT TO DO WITH CHILDHOOD?

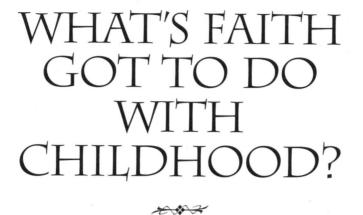

Since the fall of 1989, the Search Institute, a Minneapolis-based research organization, has been exploring what kinds of experiences and personal qualities contribute to healthy adolescent development. Approximately 400,000 American young people in grades 6 through 12 have filled out the institute's survey over the last decade. From these data, researchers have concluded that the presence or absence of a set of forty "developmental assets" in adolescents' lives is key to predicting whether these young people will engage in unhealthy behaviors (drug and alcohol use, early sexual activity, violence, suicide attempts, and so on) or avoid such behaviors.

ONE REASON FAITH MATTERS

Number 19 among these assets is one the researchers define as "kids spend one or more hours each week in religious services or participating in spiritual activities." Furthermore, several of the twenty "internal" assets that this ongoing study identifies—values like integrity, caring, and responsibility—are behaviors commonly associated with faithful living. It would seem that childhood practices and attitudes of faithfulness not only nurture spirituality but contribute to the well-being of children and thus to the well-being of society.

By the researchers' accounting, only four to six out of every ten youth surveyed have these particular assets in their lives. And only 8 percent of the entire survey sample has more than thirty of the forty assets identified as important in young people's lives. That's only 32,000 out of 400,000 teenagers who have experienced an asset-rich environment in their childhood. If more children and adults were engaged in exploring together the meaning of faith for their lives and values, this number would likely go up. That's because many of the twenty "external" assets named in the study are related to the creation of supportive relationships among children and adults and to the ways in which children use time constructively. Spiritual journeys are communal undertakings that require energy and attentiveness from those who participate in them. Faith, then, is significant for childhood because it is the place where spiritual journeys begin and healthy young (and older) lives are nurtured and sustained.

TRADITIONAL WAYS OF DEFINING FAITH

Religious traditions have approached the concept of faith in varied ways, depending on the particular concerns of those responsible for determining "faithfulness" in a given context. At times, *faith* has been equated with *belief* in certain doctrines or creeds, as in the historic periods of the Crusades or the Inquisition. Some religious groups require that their members subscribe to particular interpretations of scripture or avoid some behaviors that are considered immoral if they are to be counted among the faithful. Faith has also been defined by some as the demonstration of particular political or cultural allegiances. This means of measuring faith has been apparent in the religious conflicts surrounding Northern Ireland, Kosovo, and the Middle East. Both perspectives presume that faith is the work of human beings—a way people define what is true or morally right. Children would be expected to accept and follow the teachings of their tradition or risk correction and perhaps even punishment if they should stray from the religious "truths" of their community.

The faithfulness of individuals has also been measured by their willingness to suffer martyrdom, as the early Christians or the persecuted founders of Islam did. Indigenous peoples in Latin American and elsewhere have been enslaved by religious ideals that have equated faith with submission to earthly authorities. African Americans and women know only too well the limitations that the notion of "faith as submissiveness" can enforce on certain classes of people. Even children's participation in religious institutions has been truncated by the assumption that their obedience to parents and other adults is their primary expression of faithfulness.

Particularly problematic for children has been the way in which religious educators have used developmental theories of faith development to equate faith with a cognitive understanding of religious concepts. Some contemporary behavioral scientists have suggested that children younger than twelve must be understood as "prereligious" because such children lack the intellectual capacity to reflect rationally on their spiritual experiences. These scholars assume that authentic spirituality requires the ability to articulate some explanation or interpretation of what one is experiencing. According to this interpretation of the developmentalist perspective, faith is something that children only acquire as they mature and become capable of assenting to particular ideas about or interpretations of the religious life. In many ways, this perspective is simply another version of the first two definitions of faith: (1) the belief in certain doctrines and (2) a demonstration of particular cultural allegiances. It suggests that faith is an outcome of proper human development rather than human development being only one factor in how persons experience and express faith during their lifetimes.

A NEW DEFINITION

I would like to propose a different understanding of faith—one that doesn't depend on particular human capabilities or beliefs. My definition is this:

Faith is a gift from God.

It is not a set of beliefs; nor is it a well-developed cognitive understanding of all things spiritual.

It is an act of grace, in which God chooses to be in relationship with humanity.

This definition begins with what is beyond human understanding—the mystery Christians and Jews call God and Muslims call Allah. It presumes that God seeks relationship with us long before we begin to wonder about God. It also claims that God graciously loves and cares for all people—infants, children, teens, adults—regardless of their mental ability to understand the myriad human ideas about the nature and activity of God in the world. We might say that faith is God's presence within us—God's spirit that orients us in some unfathomable way to a love of God and of each other. Our response to this faith—this presence—is our faithfulness.

This understanding of faith is not peculiar to me. The early Christian saint—Saint Augustine—wrote about the role of God's grace in his fourth-century work *Confessions*. In a fascinating account of his conversion to Christianity, Augustine tells the story of hearing a neighbor child chanting, "Take up and read; Take up and read." Augustine interpreted these words as a message from God to pick up his Bible and read the first passage he saw there. The words Augustine read succeeded in breaking through his unsuccessful philosophical ponderings about the existence of God to touch the central questions about the meaning of life that Augustine held in his heart. He realized that God was already in relationship with him and his concerns, even though he did not believe in God.

The Jewish tradition has a similar understanding of God rooted in its concept of "covenant." In all the stories of divine-human covenant—making in the Jewish scriptures, the first partner to act is God. It is God who approaches Noah and who sets a rainbow in the sky as a sign of commitment to future generations. It is God who invites Abram to view the stars as a sign of God's everlasting covenant with the people of Israel. God also recalls the earlier covenants in raising up Moses to deliver the people out of Egypt—and so on throughout Jewish biblical history.

Many religious mystics and theologians over the ages have also embraced the idea that God first reaches out to humanity and that persons often encounter God in ways unfathomable to the usual workings of the human mind. Martin Luther, the sixteenth-century Christian reformer, coined the term *theodidacta* to describe how a person seeking to live a spiritual life must be one "taught by God" if he or she is to have a relationship with God. It was not until the Enlightenment and the Western world's consequent emphasis on rational thinking that theologies rooted in grace (those in which God's gracious actions toward humanity receive primary attention) were supplanted by theologies rooted in belief (those in which the human responses of understanding and acceptance become primary).

However, the Western religious preference for rationalism in the last three centuries did not obliterate the tension between grace

---

Being Taught by God

Martin Luther derived his idea that faithful persons need to be *theodidacti* (persons taught by God) from his careful reading of the Hebrew and Christian scriptures. The Hebrew prophet Isaiah declared to the Israelites, "All your children shall be taught by the Lord, and great shall be the prosperity of your children" (Isaiah 54:13). The later prophet, Jeremiah, spoke of how God would put God's teachings in every person's heart (Jeremiah 31:33–34), and the Christian gospel writer, John, recalled these words when he wrote, "It is written in the prophets, 'And they shall all be taught by God'" (John 6:45). When we think of our children and ourselves as *theodidacti* who have been gifted with faith by a gracious God, we stand with a long line of people whom God has embraced as spiritual learners through the ages.

5

and belief in the spiritual lives of people and communities. This tension continues to be played out in Christian traditions in the diverse practices of baptism that mark various denominations. Some denominations practice infant baptism, which points toward God's gracious acceptance of young children into the faith community long before cognitive understanding is possible or expected. These traditions then invite young people to "confirm" their faith when they are older and (presumably) better able to understand the beliefs and practices of their religious tradition. (All Jewish traditions follow a similar path of marking membership in the faith community through the *bris* or naming ceremony for infants and later the bar or bat mitzvah celebration of adolescence.) Others practice "believer's" baptism, which emphasizes a person's rational and free choice to respond to God's grace and affiliate with the community of faith. These groups may offer parents of young children an opportunity to dedicate their children to God and themselves to raising their children within the faith community and in accordance with its beliefs.

My call for defining faith as a gift from God rather than a set of beliefs or a well-developed cognitive understanding of all things spir-

Defining Faith and Faithfulness

Faith is a gift from God. It is neither a particular set of beliefs nor a well-developed cognitive understanding of all things spiritual. It is an act of grace in which God chooses to be in relationship with humanity. It comes to us in and through all our senses.

Faithfulness is a human response to God's gift of faith. It is a disposition that welcomes God's presence and seeks God's teaching. It is our age-appropriate attempt to let God's love permeate all of our senses and guide our thoughts and behavior. A faith tradition helps us recognize God's presence within us and respond faithfully.

itual is, then, an attempt to encourage us to take seriously this tension from the "grace" side of the equation so that children are recognized as fully religious beings from birth. If we hold this definition of faith as an act of grace, then we make room for children to be actual people of faith rather than just potential people of faith in need of further development before they can truly engage in a spiritual life. If faith is not something we do but something we are given by God, then anyone can be a recipient of faith and respond with faithfulness, even if that person is incapable of rational reasoning. Receiving faith becomes something different from acquiring a particular understanding of who God is or what God is doing in the world. Instead, God's gracious gift of faith comes to us and to our children through all our senses and experiences.

Faith as Multisensory Experience

The Jewish and Christian scriptures emphasize this multisensory relationship of the divine with humanity. They repeatedly tell of God choosing to act in ways that highlight a person's or community's inability to make cognitive sense of God's activity. For instance, in the story of Moses and the burning bush, a Hebrew man named Moses is working as a shepherd when he sees a bush that is blazing with fire but hasn't burned up. Moses is intrigued by this phenomenon, especially when God begins calling his name from that very bush. God tells Moses to remove his sandals because the ground around the bush is holy ground. God then continues talking to Moses, explaining that the Israelites need someone to lead them out of slavery in Egypt and that God has selected Moses for the job. Moses protests, but God continues to press the point, instructing Moses to tell the Egyptian pharaoh to let the Israelites go. Eventually, Moses asks for God's name, to which God replies, "I Am Who I Am," and gives Moses further instruction about how the escape from Egypt will be accomplished.

What drew Moses' attention to God was that the bush was burning, but it was not consumed. That burning bush didn't make sense, and the directions God gave Moses from that burning bush struck

7

Moses as equally irrational. No one, least of all the Egyptian pharaoh, was going to believe that God had chosen a nomadic shepherd to free the Hebrew people from slavery. Even Moses' attempt to elicit a rationally acceptable explanation for what was happening by asking for God's name fell short of providing an easily understood authority. For the name that came back to Moses was a name that defied human understanding. "I Am that I Am," replied God. It is as if God were saying, "Moses, your faithful interpretation of my words and actions depends on my call of you, not your understanding of me."

We can also see in the familiar accounts of the events of the Christian Holy Week (the week before Easter) how the human longing for a savior who would act in ways we think sensible led to the

A Multisensory Encounter with God

A closer look at the story of Moses and the burning bush can help you (and your children) better understand how God relates to people through all their senses. Read the following passage from the book of Exodus to yourself or aloud with your school-age children. As you read, challenge one another to notice the ways in which Moses encounters God physically (through the senses), emotionally (through feelings), and socially (through his culture, family, and tradition) in this story.

> Moses was keeping the flock of his father-in-law Jethro, the priest of Midian; he led his flock beyond the wilderness, and came to Horeb, the mountain of God. There the angel of the Lord appeared to him in a flame of fire out of a bush; he looked, and the bush was blazing, yet it was not consumed. Then Moses said, "I must turn aside and look at this great sight, and see why the bush is not burned up." When the Lord saw that he had turned aside to see, God called

crucifixion of Jesus two thousand years ago as a heretic and threat to communal order. The account of Jesus' resurrection from the dead directly challenges the disciples and our usual ways of perceiving and assessing truth. As the Apostle Paul said in his first letter to the Corinthians, the idea that God would act through death to bring new life seemed like foolishness to the Greeks, who valued cognitive ability most highly of all human attributes. Left to sort out what had happened according to their own cognitive processes, the disciples presumed that Jesus was dead and, with him, their hopes that he was the messiah. God, through the resurrection, gave them the ability to imagine other ways of faithfully interpreting God's activity in the world—ways they couldn't begin to puzzle out through reasoning.

to him out of the bush, "Moses, Moses!" And he said, "Here I am." Then he said, "Come no closer! Remove the sandals from your feet for the place on which you are standing is holy ground." He said further, "I am the God of your father, the God of Abraham, the God of Isaac, and the God of Jacob." And Moses hid his face, for he was afraid to look at God.

Notice the variety of ways that Moses encounters God's presence in addition to his cognitive curiosity about the unconsumed bush. Physically, he encounters God with all his senses: smelling smoke, looking, hearing, speaking, and touching holy ground with his feet. Emotionally, he wavers between awe and fear, amazed by the bush and afraid to see God before him. Socially, he responds to his name and relates to the history of his religious tradition. If we continued reading this story in Exodus, chapter 3, we would discover just how worried Moses was about his reputation. Even in the brief excerpt, we see how Moses learns about and interprets God's presence through a wide range of activities, emotions, recollections, and abilities.

Faith as a Transformative Gift

If we accept that faith is a divine gift present from our birth, not something we create for ourselves, then engaging in a life of faithfulness means responding at every age to God's gift with actions rooted in the faith we have been given. Faith informs and transforms the spiritual lives of children and adults. Like a bit of yeast that leavens a whole loaf of bread, it modifies the lives of those to whom it is given. It affects and alters all of life's ingredients. Yet the transformation of flour, sugar, water, and other ingredients into bread dough requires mixing and kneading the yeast into the other ingredients. The yeast can be present without expression, but that is not the purpose of the yeast. It is added to the dough so that the mixture might be transformed into bread. In like manner, faith is given us by God so that it may transform our lives as we faithfully interpret God's words and deeds in our context.

Our role, then, as parents and adults who work with children, is to introduce and support spiritual practices that serve to mix and knead faith into the dough of children's lives. Such practices include worship, prayer, contemplation, study, confession and reconciliation, witness (testimony) and service—all of which I will discuss in further detail in later chapters. But before we can introduce such practices, we need to understand how children of various ages and stages of development are likely to experience a relationship with God. Let me highlight for you now some of the implications human development has for children's spiritual lives.

HUMAN DEVELOPMENT AND THE EXPRESSION OF FAITH

To say that children are people of faith is not to say that their expressions of faith are identical to adult expressions. Although faith is not dependent on or beholden to human development, the expression of faith is affected by physical, cognitive, emotional, and social development. And developmentally, human beings are predictably different as they move through the life cycle. Infants, toddlers, preschoolers, and elementary-age children each have different abilities and primary activities from those of older youths and adults. Unfortunately, the hierarchical nature of many developmental charts, with their linear construction and emphasis on upward movement toward "optimal" adult functioning, has distracted us from the very real capabilities that children have *as children.* Instead of using human development theories to focus on children's deficiencies, as has been the tendency in contemporary parenting and religious education literature, we need to use this research to help us, as adults, understand how children can, in fact, be faithful throughout childhood.

Infants and young toddlers both symbolize the mysterious and miraculous nature of the spiritual realm and experience the love of God through positive relationships with adult caregivers. They come from the womb accustomed to having their needs met by some means beyond themselves, and they actively seek to be in relationship with those they perceive will respond to their smiles and cries. They spend their time "overseeing" and "overhearing" the wider community in which they live and incorporating their experiences into a sense of personal and communal identity. They populate their evolving image of community with the people, characters, and objects around them. The presence or absence of spiritually significant objects, stories, rituals, and practices affects whether the very young child incorporates these specific signs and narratives of spirituality into his or her fundamental worldview.

Young children's reasoning is based on perception and intuition. Most children construct some kind of God concept from their parents and other significant adults before entering the preschool years. The concept of God at this age serves much the same purpose as the toddler's blankie or teddy bear. It is a transitional object, say some psychologists—an image that works like a security blanket to satisfy a child's desire for constancy and predictability. The ways that young children describe God also reflect their growing awareness of the social structures of their environment. Even when adults emphasize nontraditional images of God or are generally nonreligious, preschool children typically identify God as an old, white man with a beard.

What's Faith Got to Do with Childhood?

They do this in part because they have recognized the cultural messages embedded in the media and many social institutions that depict such men as powerful. They also tend to associate the magical presence of Santa Claus with God, who, they assume, must be magical as well. One of the most important spiritual needs of preschool children is the freedom to discover and create spiritual images of God, heaven, and death that express their evolving feelings and comprehension of the world around them. Another is the need to create or participate in meaningful rituals and practices that acknowledge the presence of God in the ordinary events of their lives.

In the preschool and early elementary years, children use pretend play to interiorize the symbol systems of their community, including the religious ideas to which they are exposed. Such play allows children to appropriate and modify the symbols they intuit or perceive according to their own understanding of their life experiences. Around ages six or seven, children become deeply responsive to narratives that might explain their lives and their world. This occurs in large part because this is when children are learning to read and write, so their fascination with deciphering and replicating words affects all aspects of their being.

Until approximately age nine, children continue to imbue God with magical qualities. Their propensity for fantasizing easily allows for the idea that God works miracles by altering the usual conditions of nature, causing it to rain on demand or making someone who is dead return to life. They continue to be filled with awe and wonder at simple things like the flickering of a lighted candle or an ant carrying a leaf back to the anthill, and it is not a stretch for them to attribute such amazing actions to the work of a Creator with superpowers. What matters to them is that God, like all authorities in their lives, should use God's power fairly. They expect "good" people to do well and "bad" people to be punished. For many children, especially preteens, God is also a confidant to whom they may talk at length about their ideas and troubles. Spiritual practices for children in this age group need to take into account their attentiveness to narratives, their concern for fairness, and their desire to believe and confide in a powerful and magical being.

Between the ages of ten and twelve, children become less engaged with magical thinking and begin to take a more "scientific" approach to spirituality and God. The kind of cognitive development that typically occurs in this age group moves them from simple cause-effect reasoning about fairness to more complicated and abstract ideas about what is right and just. They become more aware of multiple and competing social and religious perspectives from which to choose their own positions. We might characterize them as "spiritual inquirers," interested in investigating the claims of their own and other traditions and naming their own beliefs. They need spiritual practices that nurture and affirm this inquisitive mode.

This brief overview of some of the ways children at different stages of development experience and engage in the spiritual life only begins to hint at the opportunities parents and other adults have to nurture and sustain children's spirituality. I will return in Chapter Six to the various ways our growing understanding of human development assists us as we share our children's spiritual journeys.

Spiritual Formation and Children

What I have been presenting in this chapter, albeit in brief form, is a general understanding of spiritual formation that keeps coming back to three central themes. One theme is that faith is given to human beings, including children, as a gracious act of God. The second is that faith informs and transforms human lives and that spiritual practices facilitate faith's transformative work because they link us with God. The third is that our best human response to faith is "faithfulness," in which we live in ways that suggest the faith God has given us has affected all aspects of our life fully.

In order for us to make sense of how these three important aspects of an understanding of faith and faithfulness can most effectively shape our efforts to nurture children's spirituality, we need to consider what other normative concepts might help us further define our understanding of "faith-full-ness." I propose that exploring such concepts as belonging, thanksgiving, giftedness, hospitality, under-

Age-Related Aspects of Faithfulness

Birth to Three Years
- Experience God's love embodied in caregivers
- "Overhear" and "oversee" the life of their spiritual community
- Develop a spiritual sense of community and personal identity in relation to the signs and symbols around them
- Relate to the idea of God as they relate to a beloved stuffed animal or blanket: as something that provides security
- Provide an image of the mysterious and creative power of God for adults

Three to Eight Years
- Interpret their spiritual experience using perception and intuition
- View God as a miracle worker
- Apply their growing awareness of the social structures of their environment to religious ideas

standing, and hope will provide us with some ideas about what faithful living might look like for both children and adults. Although it is somewhat misleading to take them as separate categories because of their interrelatedness, let's look briefly at each concept, in no particular order of significance.

Belonging

Our definition of faith implies that all people, whether children or adults, belong to the family of God because of God's actions rather than our own. Some religious traditions even use the metaphor of adoption to illustrate the way in which we become part of God's family. Just as adoptive parents choose to extend their love to a child born into another household or residing in another culture, welcoming and

- Use pretend play to explore the ideas and symbols of their spiritual community
- Are deeply responsive to religious narratives
- Need the freedom to discover and create images that express their evolving connections between their spiritual experiences and their social world

Nine to Twelve Years
- Interested in investigating the claims of religious traditions and naming their own beliefs
- Aware of multiple and competing social and religious perspectives from which to choose
- Need adult assistance to develop a thoughtful inquisitiveness in relation to their spiritual experiences
- Highly sensitive to adult hypocrisy and expect those around them to live by their values and commitments

caring for this little "stranger" as their own, God embraces each member of the human race as beloved and accepted. Nurturing the spiritual lives of children, then, requires us to consider how we will communicate to them a sense of their belonging in the household of faith. How will they recognize that they belong to God as well as to the human family and its many communities?

Thanksgiving

The theme of being "informed and transformed" by the gift of faith suggests that it is appropriate for God to expect that we will live our lives with a sense of gratitude for God's gracious gift. The common usage of the doxology words, "Praise God from whom all blessings flow" in Christian worship offers a clue as to the form this thankful

What's Faith Got to Do with Childhood?

response might take. Implicit in one petition of the Lord's Prayer ("Give us this day our daily bread") is another clue. With these words, children and adults learn to pray daily for God's provision of what they need for the day rather than approach life with a sense of entitlement. The Jewish mealtime prayer, "Blessed are you, Lord God, who brings forth the fruit of the earth," acknowledges a similar gratitude for God's provision of our needs. This aspect of faithfulness raises a question about how adults cultivate thankfulness in children's lives in such a way that children learn an appropriate dependence on God rather than the heavily emphasized cultural values of self-reliance and autonomy. An attitude of thanksgiving for all the good things we receive in life does not require the cultivation of a kind of dependence based in passivity but an appreciation for the interrelatedness of life systems that transcends a particular person's role within them.

Giftedness

Human beings are created by God, with specific and valuable gifts and abilities necessary for the wholeness of the world. One need not subscribe to a literal religious interpretation of the biblical creation story to believe that every living creature is wondrously and uniquely made. Children are no less gifted than adults, although their gifts and abilities may manifest themselves differently at various ages and stages of their lives. If we believe that all our gifts and abilities are needed for the world to be whole and at peace, then the idea of giftedness raises the question of how adults can encourage children to identify and use their particular gifts and abilities for the development and well-being of the world. Social science research can assist us in this task by providing information about human development and behavior to guide our work.

Hospitality

The concept of hospitality reinforces the values of belonging, giving thanks for the gift of faith, and extending the fruits of our giftedness to others. All persons are called to share the gifts they have been given so that God's realm may come in all its fullness. In order for children to fulfill this destiny, adults must work to create spaces in which children experience the connections between their actions and the rest of the workings of the world. Parents and others who work with children must help children name injustice and cultivate within children a desire to live compassionately. Thus hospitality is about nurturing children's ability and desire to welcome the stranger as they have been welcomed. It involves assisting children as they live out their sense of thanksgiving through caring for the others on whom they depend. And it means encouraging children to cultivate their gifts for more than their own personal development.

Understanding

Both children and adults seek spiritual awareness by reflecting, as they are able, on their spiritual experiences. Reflection generally happens through some process of exploring or questioning one's experience. An infant who continually mouths a toy is reflecting, albeit without the cognition of an adult, on the properties of that toy: its taste, texture, shape, and so on. The repeated question, "Why?" of a two-year-old is an attempt to reflect on the physical or social systems of the child's environment. School-age children begin to use more recognizable forms of systematic inquiry as they study a subject or phenomenon. To nurture spiritual understanding, we need to encourage children to explore their spiritual experiences and to ask what these experiences mean for them. What does it mean for the Jewish child that he or she celebrates Shabbat with the rest of the family each Friday evening? How does the Christian child interpret the family practice of saying a prayer before each meal? Children and adults need to communicate their reflections on these experiences to one another and the burden for creating times and places for good communication on these and other topics falls to adults.

Hope

An important aspect of spirituality is that it orients our lives around the expectation that there is something more to human existence than what we most obviously can see or know. Particularly in times of difficulty, children and adults long for miracles, for words and actions that seem impossible, to occur. The concept of hope points us toward the mysteries of the universe and provides a way for us to find joy and anticipate the unexpected. It also encourages us to think outside the box to new ways of seeing and acting in the world rather than those most commonly observed around us. Children, perhaps more easily than adults, dwell in states of hopefulness and imaginative possibilities. In this sense, they may nurture us as much or more than we nurture them as we sojourn on our spiritual paths together. Our primary task may be to open our ears to their imaginings and affirm their hopeful engagement with the world. We can also work intentionally at introducing children each and every day to new mysteries of God and God's universe.

FROM FAITH TO FAITHFULNESS

Faith is a given for children—indeed, for us all. But faithfulness is something we cultivate as we live together as spiritual people in relation with God. One of the challenges of being and working with children is to remember that they are already gifted with faith while also remembering that they do not automatically acquire the words and actions to express that faith. Cultivating the spiritual lives of children takes effort on the part of parents, teachers, and adult friends. We must pay attention to the messages we send children about their place in the world, their relationship to the holy, and their responsibility to contribute to the well-being of the human community. We must be sure that children have reasons to give thanks by providing for their basic physical, emotional, and social needs and protecting them from harm as best we are able. We must resist the temptation to label children— "the quiet one," "the hyper one," "the flirt"—and instead look for the particular gifts and abilities each child possesses. (And yes, this can be a challenge when we're walking a colicky baby, worn out from trying to keep up with a rambunctious toddler, or contending with a defiant ten-year-old!) We must practice hospitality toward both strangers and friends, so our children will know what genuine hospitality looks and

Belonging being embraced by God and a community of faith as beloved and accepted

Thanksgiving living with a sense of gratitude for the gift of faith and God's provision of one's daily needs

Giftedness knowing that each person is wondrously and uniquely made, with gifts and abilities to contribute to the community

Hospitality sharing one's gifts and welcoming the gifts of others so that God's vision of a just and peaceful world can be realized

Understanding reflecting on one's spiritual experiences in order to become aware of how they shape one's life and commitments

Hope expecting that there is something more to human existence than what we presently see or know

feels like. We must talk about why we make the choices we make and do the things we do so that our children witness our self-reflection and can follow our lead. We must welcome their questions, even when we are tired of explaining (although it is perfectly legitimate to defer them to a more appropriate or relaxed time of discussion). More than anything else, we must live as people who imagine that something more exists than just those things we can see and feel. We needn't be able to explain exactly what does exist beyond ourselves and the sensible world—the holy is not meant to be neatly defined in human terms—but we must allow for it and seek relationship with it. Following Moses' lead, we and the children we love and care for can open all our senses to the spiritual realm and, in doing so, discover that God is eager to join us in the spiritual adventure we call life.

Chapter 2

CREATING A SPIRITUAL WORLD FOR CHILDREN TO INHABIT

❧❖❧

When my older son David was three, he talked about heaven as if it were a perfect replica of his nursery school room. He anticipated spending time in God's "block corner" should he go to heaven someday. He also believed a game of catch with me involved a third player, God, who was responsible for sending the ball on its downward arc after I had thrown the ball into the air toward David. This personification of gravity allowed him to bring God into his world in a sensible way. My daughter Paula, when four, would repeat key religious words she knew—"hosanna," "alleluia," "Jesus"—as she attempted to participate in congregational hymn singing. It did not bother her that nearby adults were singing different words. She had identified for herself a set of significant terms and was using them to express her desire for connection with God. Michael, my younger son, insisted at the age of four that a lowercase "t" was not a letter but a cross, because his primary awareness of that written shape was as a religious symbol rather than a linguistic one.

CHILDREN'S WORLDVIEWS

Each of these examples demonstrates the way in which the cultural and religious experiences of a young child interact to shape that child's activities in and interpretations of the world. From the moment of birth, one of a child's primary tasks is to create a world in which to live. A newborn is only familiar with the world of the womb: darkness, constant nourishment, sensations of floating in a confined space, the whoosh-whoosh of the maternal heartbeat, the rhythm of maternal movements. The lights, sounds, and other sensory experiences of the birthing process and neonatal period require babies to begin reorienting themselves to a new world.

Adults in the newborn's world support this adjustment, in part by engaging in practices and creating rituals reminiscent of the child's former world. For example, the practice of swaddling a baby tightly in a blanket recreates the close embrace of the womb; front packs and baby slings allow the child to be cradled close to the heart and carried to the rhythm of a parent's steps. And nursing "on demand" minimizes sensations of hunger that are unknown before birth. The nightly ritual of a warm bath, followed by feeding and rocking the baby to sleep, provides the comfortable sensations of floating and of the rhythmic movement experienced during gestation.

Other practices and rituals introduce infants to their new world. Colorful toys that make a variety of sounds capture their attention and tune their eyes and ears to look and listen. The family bedtime ritual signals that the time for an extended period of sleep in one's bed has come. The prompt response of caregivers to the child's cries teaches that this new world also meets one's needs but in a different way from the former world. As babies grow older, they seek more and more knowledge about their new world. A favorite toddler pastime is naming the objects around them. They incessantly wonder, "What is it?" and expect the adults around them to name item after item as they point to each one. They are in the process of incorporating all these things into their own picture of the world and how it works. Things that they do not see, hear, taste, smell, or feel simply do not exist as a part of their universe.

CHILDREN'S ENVIRONMENTS

Before our first child was born, my husband and I spent many hours thinking about how we would decorate the baby's room. We didn't have much money to dedicate to this endeavor. In fact, we didn't really have a room—just a corner of what was technically the dining room in our old-fashioned one-bedroom duplex. These limitations, however, didn't stop us from flipping through magazines, browsing through baby stores, and visiting neighborhood yard sales as we hunted for just the right pictures, curtains, and crib bumper pad to welcome our little one. We knew, both somewhat instinctively and because the baby books told us so, that the images babies encounter in the first years of life make an impression on them. We wanted our child to encounter a lively and joyous collection of characters and scenes as he lay in his crib and surveyed his surroundings. So we hung curtains with Mickey Mouse and his friends sailing in colorful hot-air balloons on the windows and set a lamp shaped like Mickey holding a bouquet of balloons on the dresser. An aunt donated a bright yellow Big Bird bank, and a blue, furry Cookie Monster soon followed. We awaited the birth of our son, secure in the sense that he would come to know and appreciate these characters traditionally associated with American childhood and that his world with us would be more interesting and happier because of the presence of these cultural icons. And indeed, like millions of children before him, he took delight in making friends with them.

WHO ARE THE PEOPLE IN OUR CHILDREN'S NEIGHBORHOODS?

Our children's love for the imaginary worlds represented by Mickey and Minnie, Big Bird, Winnie-the-Pooh, Thomas the Tank Engine, Madeleine, and other popular children's characters offers us some insight into how children also learn to embrace the characters and images of a religious world. First of all, children relate to characters and images they see frequently and therefore recognize as familiar.

23

Mickey and his friends are almost *everywhere* a child goes, so our little ones accept them as an essential part of the world. They can't remember a time when they didn't "know" that Mickey Mouse is Mickey Mouse—they way they know that Mommy is Mommy or recognize that the family pet belongs to the household. Catching sight of Elmo in a store window or on television is like reconnecting with an old friend. Carrying a stuffed Pooh around provides comfort and reassurance when other aspects of the child's world seem less certain and predictable.

For children to develop a similar relationship with the images and characters of their faith tradition, they must see these images and characters frequently. Otherwise, the characters of their faith stories are like distant relatives who come to visit once or twice a year. They are essentially strangers, to whom children react with disinterest, suspicion, or tentative engagement.

Second, the spiritual characters in a child's world need to have names and personalities. A friend's daughter, who is not quite two years old, delights in being asked, "What does Mickey say?" Her reply: "Oh, boy!" in an almost perfect imitation of Mickey's well-known voice. It is her intimate knowledge of the Disney character that fuels her delight in talking about and acting like him. Children need a similar knowledge of the characters that people their own faith tradition. They need to hear about King David, who played the harp, practiced shooting arrows with his best friend Jonathan, and refused to be scared by the bully Goliath. They need to sing and dance with Miriam, who played the tambourine as God led the Israelites out of Egypt and toward the promised land. They need to hear the stories of Jesus calling his disciples frequently enough that, if asked, "What did Jesus say?" they might reply, "Follow me." Only when they know enough details about these people of faith to make them easily recognizable by their attributes will they think of them again and again as they work to make sense of their world.

Several years ago, while in seminary, I taught a group of two-year-olds during a weeklong vacation church school program. The theme for the week was the story of Moses. One of our daily activities was a toddler finger play that went, "God said to Pharaoh, 'Let my people go.' But Pharaoh said, 'No, no no!'" During the first half of the finger play, the children and I would shake our fingers just like a chastising parent. Then we would switch to shaking our heads "no" during the second section. The children loved this finger play because it mimicked their real-life experiences, and many parents reported that their toddlers were still reciting this rhythm after several months.

What I did not anticipate at the time was the lingering effect this activity would have on at least one of the children. I learned about it ten years later, when a former seminary colleague stopped me at a conference to say that his preteen son had been talking about a finger play he remembered from his toddler days; he recalled how the words had come back to him as an example of the times God expects different things from people from what they want to give. My friend's son was reflecting on how easy it had been to be contrary when he was younger and how much more personal responsibility he had for making good choices as a twelve-year-old. A simple church school activity had made this biblical story come alive for him in a way that reinforced the importance of the story and its characters for his understanding of how the world worked. And so, a decade after this child first heard about the Exodus, his graphic recollection of Pharaoh's and God's words remained a powerful part of his worldview.

Not all moments in which we can recognize a spiritual connection between children's worldviews and the stories of their faith tradition carry such moral significance as with my friend's son. Sometimes these connections simply remind us that our children use what they know to explain what seems different or strange to them. While watching a Christmas pageant enacted by the residents of a nursing home, my daughter exclaimed, "Look Mom, she's just like Sarah!" when the elderly woman playing Mary pushed her walker onto the platform. This unusual staging of the story about Jesus' birth triggered my daughter's memory of another biblical story in which the elderly Abraham and Sarah learned that they would become parents for the first time. My daughter, being used to Christmas pageants in which Mary is played by a girl or young woman, shifted her surprise into understanding by linking the two biblical stories around their common theme: giving birth to a baby promised by God. Not only did she solve the "mystery" of how an elderly woman could play Mary but she grasped for a moment the sense that God works across time and space in different but related ways. Such discoveries help children imagine that God is present in their world, too, just as God was part of the worlds of Sarah and Mary.

Children begin borrowing ideas from their environment to make sense of their world at a very young age. Toddlers and preschoolers perceive the dominant values of their culture well before they can articulate those beliefs or assess whether they are appropriate or inappropriate. An African American toddler boy who repeatedly watches cartoon videos in which the "good guys" with light-colored skin always beat the "bad guys" with dark-colored skin concludes from this observation that light-skinned people are good and dark-skinned people are bad. (A Caucasian child comes to a similar conclusion.) When he is four or five and becomes aware of his own skin color, he will likely experience a tension between his sense of himself as good and his cultural observation that dark-colored skin belongs to bad guys. His white peers will also be more likely to label him as bad when trouble erupts on the playground.

Similarly, very young children can learn values that contradict the dominant culture's belief structures. A toddler girl who frequently stands on a chair beside her father as he washes dishes learns through observation that housework is something fathers do, and when she engages in pretend play, she may pretend to be a father washing dishes. Because she does not yet associate fatherhood with biological sex, she has little difficulty imaging herself as the daddy working at the sink. When she is older and capable of making gender distinctions, she may even identify dishwashing as a masculine job, based on her personal observation of her father's behavior.

The enduring strength of the assumptions that young children make about the world based on their observations has become powerfully apparent to me through conversations I have had with preschool and early elementary children over the past decade. When I began my last position as a parish pastor, I asked a group of children ages three to six what they thought about having me as their new minister. A five-year-old girl responded, "I'm glad you're a girl, be-

Childhood Cultures

Young children have two important strengths operating for them as they learn about the world and their role in it: keen observational powers and imagination. As they experience the people, images, and activities around them, they tune in to feelings, voice inflections, gestures, patterns, associations, and implicit norms and rules. They then incorporate these aspects of their experience into their social interactions and pretend play. They "try on" the roles and behaviors of people and characters with which they are familiar. A minister told me about a visit to her office from a mother and her preschool daughter. As the pastor and mother talked, the child began to play in a corner of the room, reenacting the healing service she had participated in with her parents and faith community the past evening. She lined up a group of stuffed animals, talking about their ailments as she put them into place. Then she asked the minister if there was some oil she could use to "bless" the animals and help them feel better. Told she would need to pretend to have oil, she began to touch each animal on the head and say brief prayers for it to get well. Her actions demonstrated the incorporation of her experience of the congregation's practice of anointing the sick into her own cultural identity as a "normal" aspect of human life and community.

cause my mom said we might get a boy minister, and I don't think boys can be real ministers!" Several other children nodded in agreement at her words. These children had grown up in a congregation led solely by female pastors; they considered female clergy the norm and were skeptical of male "imposters." Even their parents' assurances that men could be and were "real" ministers had not convinced them to set aside their personal observations.

Creating a Spiritual World for Children to Inhabit

A conversation with my oldest son when he was seven also illustrates the power of a child's early perceptions of his world. David endured several painful medical tests in the month proceeding his third birthday, including a bone marrow biopsy. The day before his younger sister's third birthday, he turned to me at the dinner table and asked when his sister was going to have her "really big lab test." Surprised, I asked what he meant. "You know," he said, "that bone thing like I had." I discovered that he had defined his experience with the bone marrow biopsy as something normative for all children turning three years old. He assumed that all his friends had a similar experience in their background. When he realized that his experience had been unusual, he spent several weeks working through the meaning of this revelation for his own sense of self. The experiences young children have, the images they see, and the stories they hear become long-lasting frameworks on which they construct their perceptions of reality.

LIVING IN TWO CULTURES

What I have come to realize as a parent and a religious educator is that my children are living in two cultures. One culture is that of our local community: our neighborhood, schools, network of friends, and life in a Midwestern city. The other culture is that of our religious community: our family spiritual practices, local congregation, and wider church events. Both of these cultures contribute to my children's particular understanding of what the world is like, how it works, and who they are in it. But one of these cultures—that of the general community environment—has much greater potential to dominate my children's thinking because, like the commercial icons who represent it, my children encounter it almost everywhere. I don't have to wonder whether this culture will influence my children's lives; my concern has to be with how much power this culture has relative to the second culture—that of our religious community. I have to help my children negotiate the overlaps and tensions between these two worlds so they can become genuinely bicultural.

Acculturation

Jean Phinney researches and writes about the psychology of bicultural identity among ethnic immigrants to the United States. She begins an essay in a recent American Psychological Association volume by explaining that a person's identity as part of a minority ethnic group is created through the person's interactions with both that group and the larger cultural group within which the ethnic group resides. Over time, ethnic immigrants deal with their ethnicity in one of three ways: (1) they withdraw into stronger identification with their ethnic tradition; (2) they relinquish many of their ethnic characteristics through assimilation into the wider culture, or (3) they develop a strong identification with both cultures.

Persons who emphasize their connections with both cultures, such as second-generation Mexican immigrants who label themselves Mexican American, are considered bicultural. They demonstrate loyalty to their ethnic origins through participation in some of that culture's rituals, practices, and beliefs while adopting some of the second culture's ways of being and doing in the world. *Acculturation* is the name given to the process by which such immigrants learn the orienting stories, values, practices, and rituals in their new culture.

For adults seeking to help children flourish as spiritual beings, the religious world that gives a spiritual life substance and form is a second culture. It is a new world in which both children and the adults who sojourn with them may be immigrants. Learning to identify with this second culture requires intentional encounters with its many and varied aspects: its language, values, beliefs, practices, images, resources, and institutions. As families who are seeking a way to flourish spiritually, we may not have to leave our country of origin (as ethnic immigrants do) to find a new land in which to pursue our dreams, but we do have to open ourselves to new experiences, new ways of imagining the world, and new ways of making meaning for ourselves and our children. This allows for the kind of dynamic development necessary for the cultivation of religious identity.

Cultural Negotiation

Most adults and children already have some experience negotiating two or more different cultures because the formation of households generally brings at least two families of origin into relationship. The first Christmas after my husband and I were married, we realized that we had been raised with different assumptions about what symbol goes on the top of a Christmas tree. His family always put an angel on top; my family decorated the tree with a star. We discovered that our sense of how one *should* celebrate Christmas was, in part, tied to the replication of the traditions with which we had grown up. With two competing traditions to accommodate, we had to decide what we would do. Acculturation theory suggests we had four options: (1) one of us could choose to abandon the tradition of our family of origin and *assimilate* to the other person's family culture; (2) we could each go back to our family of origin and celebrate the holiday in our *separate* cultures; (3) we could decide not to have a Christmas tree at all and thus *marginalize* both cultures as irrelevant to our personal lives, or (4) we could *integrate* elements of our original cultures into a new household tradition of our own making. We eventually decided on the integration strategy, combining the angel tree-topper of my husband's childhood with the kind of tinsel reminiscent of my family's tradition. It took a few years, however, before our Christmas tree ceased to look a little strange to both of us because it didn't reflect fully the images we had carried from a young age.

Such cultural negotiations are even more complicated for interfaith households. A friend from graduate school shared with me her painful decision to forego a Christmas tree in her home after the birth of her first child. She and her husband, who is Jewish, had agreed that their children would be raised in the Jewish faith. They had also agreed that it was desirable for their children to be "exposed" to their mother's Christian tradition by participating in celebrations outside the home with their maternal relatives. My friend had no problem accepting these decisions intellectually, but they were harder to implement than she had expected. And what triggered the biggest difficulty? It was her inability to figure out what she should do with

REAL KIDS, REAL FAITH

her Christmas ornaments. Every year while she was growing up, her parents had given her and her siblings each a Christmas ornament that was intended to hang on their own trees once they left home. Leaving those ornaments packed away posed too great a threat to my friend's sense of her own cultural (and familial) identity. Eventually, she decided to have her children help her hang those ornaments back on their maternal grandparents' Christmas tree each year, reinforcing the separation strategy she and her husband had adopted at their marriage.

In both my own and my friend's case, our experiences of conflict between two cultures generated an intentional process of reflection and decision making geared toward a better understanding of our own identity and its meaning in relationship to others. It also generated concern for how we would construct the familial and religious cultures into which we would invite our own children. As we debated (on a minor and a major scale) which images and symbols we would incorporate into our household holiday traditions, we were engaged in decorating the spaces from which our children would draw their ideas about God and spirituality.

CREATING A SPIRITUAL WORLD AROUND THE HOLIDAYS

Religious holidays offer an easy entry point into a discussion of how we intentionally create a spiritual world for our children to inhabit. It is commonplace to decorate one's home and engage in special practices for such events. Christian families may put out nativity scenes for Christmas Eve and tuck palm branches over the mantle at the beginning of Holy Week. They may join others for caroling parties and invite extended-family members to feast with them. Jewish and interfaith Jewish-Christian families may place menorahs in the windows for Hanukah or put out special linens and china for the dining-room table at Passover. Latkes (potato pancakes), tzimmes (sweet-and-sour vegetables), and matzo ball (dumpling) soup remind taste buds that it's time to celebrate.

The particular challenge that we have as spiritual persons living in a wider culture is distinguishing between the spiritual aspects of religious holidays and the many trappings of the wider culture's celebration of these same events. What does it mean to celebrate Christmas and Hanukkah in a spiritually authentic way when one begins encountering Santa Claus decorations and Christmas gift marketing campaigns in stores well before Halloween? Christians contend with the confusion of trying to explain what Santa Claus has to do with the birth of Jesus. Jewish and interfaith families face the dilemma of inflating the traditionally minor celebration of Hanukkah in order to compete with the marketing appeal of the American Christmas. The image of Santa Claus is so powerful in our wider culture that most preschool children describe God as a kind of Santa figure without the red suit: an old man with white hair and beard and magical powers who is generally good natured unless one does something wrong. Without other images to challenge this prominent cultural icon, our children become spiritually assimilated to the values and practices associated with this Santa "god" and his rituals rather than integrate the best elements of their religious culture and the wider culture in a spiritually enlivening, bicultural identity.

In my household and religious community, we talk about the phenomenon of two Christmases as a fact we need to acknowledge explicitly with children. There is much about the Santa tradition that is fun, and we enjoy the pleasure that finding small gifts for a child's stocking or writing a letter to the North Pole brings. But we name these activities as ways we participate in a cultural tradition designed to bring happiness through telling imaginative stories and exchanging gifts with people we love. We tell our children that Santa is an idea people came up with so they could enjoy surprising one another with gifts. We talk about how much fun it is to imagine an underdog reindeer becoming a hero because his glowing red nose "saves" the holiday surprise party. (We compare the Rudolph story to that of the Ugly Duckling as well.) We celebrate with the wider culture the wonder of electric lights twinkling on rooftops and reenact the scenes from my childhood in which persons in our household take turns, from youngest to oldest, opening one gift at a time on Christmas morning until the space under the tree is empty. But we do not allow our celebration to stop here. Instead, we invite our children to engage in another set of practices related to the Christian season of Advent, a time of preparation for and expectation of the birth of the Christ child on Christmas Eve night.

We have to work harder at celebrating Advent and the spiritual meaning of Christmas than we would if we only recognized and celebrated the Santa tradition of the holiday. Beginning with the Sunday four weekends before Christmas Day, we light candles in a special wreath, read short excerpts from the scriptures that tell stories leading up to Jesus' birth, and sing hymns like "O Come, O Come Emmanuel" that remind us and our children of the other event besides Santa Claus's arrival that marks Christmas Eve. We set up several nativity scenes around our house but add the figures to the stable slowly, holding back the Christ child until the night of his birth (and the three kings until the religious celebration of their arrival at Epiphany on January 6). Sometimes we get together with other families and throw a birthday party for baby Jesus, inviting all the children in our neighborhood to bring gifts for those who, like Jesus and his family, struggle to find safe places to sleep.

My children's favorite Advent tradition is our annual family trip to the local mall's "Angel Tree," where each child picks one or two personalized ornaments off a display sponsored by a local social service agency and then goes Christmas shopping for those persons. They often select children their own ages and purchase items that they themselves would love to have as a sign of their desire to make Christmas morning as special for others as it is for them. This is a place where our tradition of keeping two Christmases comes together as one celebration. The cultural practice of giving gifts to those we love extends itself to those who are strangers through our spiritual commitment to love our neighbor as ourselves in gratitude for God's gift of love in Christ. Jewish families make similar connections between their acts of forgiveness and goodwill toward others and God's forgiveness of them in the observance of Yom Kippur. Islamic families participate in the practice of *zakat* (offering gifts to the poor) as one of the five central emphases of their religion. We can begin to help chil-

Creating a Spiritual World for Children to Inhabit

dren inhabit a spiritual world when we help them see how the holiday traditions of the wider culture are both distinct from and related to the practices of our own and others' faith traditions.

Celebrating the Spiritual Meaning of Christmas

The stores may begin hawking their wares in line with the dominant cultural celebration of Christmas well before Halloween, but there is still much that parents and other adults can do to help children discover the religious reason for the season. Phyllis Vos Wezeman and Jude Fournier, in their book *Celebrating Seasons,* suggest setting aside time—at bedtime, perhaps, or after Sunday supper—to think about and pray for the people represented by the Christmas cards the family has received. They also provide a recipe for "King's Cake," a traditional treat for celebrating the twelfth day of Christmas. Debbie O'Neal, in *Before and After Christmas,* suggests creating cards and wrapping paper designed to celebrate the concept of *joy* and provides spelling and pronunciation for the word in a dozen different languages. She also tells a variety of legends about Christmas traditions and offers activities such as the creation of *luminaria* (special candles to line one's walkway or hall), Scandinavian woven hearts (to celebrate St. Lucia Day), and a wood block nativity set. In *These Twelve Days,* James Kasperson and Marina Lachecki offer an explanation of a Christmas tradition, a scripture reference, a contemporary story, and several activity ideas for each of the twelve days of Christmas. This extended celebration of a central event in the Christian faith has the added benefit of addressing the post-December 25 blues that befall many families whose anticipation of the great day otherwise gives way to an emotional letdown once the gifts have all been unwrapped.

CREATING AN EVERYDAY SPIRITUAL WORLD

Although religious holidays help us introduce a spiritual world to our children, our greater challenge is to connect their religious imagination with the ordinary aspects of everyday life. We want children to have the sense that God is with them always and everywhere, not just when there's a party going on. This means we need to have images and practices in our households and religious institutions that call attention to God's presence in the world and offer opportunities to reflect on what it means that God is with us. The Jewish practice of placing a small case (a *mezuzah*) holding a tiny scripture scroll in the upper-right corner of the frame of their front door provides one example of how some people of faith encourage such attentiveness; the presence of this symbol and the practice of touching it with reverence reminds all who enter the house that God dwells within. Christians, drawing on their shared history with Judaism, can create a similar reminder for their homes. Some Catholic homes have a small shrine to a particular saint in their yard or garden or a crucifix hanging inside the front door. These images identify the family as "Catholic," both to outsiders and to those who live within the household. Children in these households grow up with a sense that their core identity is connected to Catholicism in some way because their religious culture is explicitly acknowledged in the intimate space of their home. The message children receive from such things as mezuzot, shrines, and crucifixes in the home is that these images are "my" images and "my family's" images. They belong to the family just as the rest of the furniture, pictures, and household items do.

Hanging in my own dining room are two framed posters. One is the sort of image common to a middle-class white household: a reproduction of Vincent Van Gogh's *Café Terrace at Night.* The other poster, however, is not a common dining-room piece. It is John August Swanson's *The Procession,* which depicts a crowd of people carrying banners with images of traditional Christian stories through the streets of a village during Holy Week. Sometimes, over breakfast or dinner, my children and I play guessing games with this poster, challenging one another to find particular story images or puzzling over a banner image that refers to a story we aren't sure we recognize. These games help my children learn the stories of our faith tradition, and the prominence of the poster in our dining room communicates the importance our family places on these stories.

Let me show you around the rest of the house so you can see some of the other ways my husband and I try to create a spiritual world for our children to inhabit. In the living room by the stereo there are CDs of classical religious music and Christian artists mixed in with James Taylor, Disney soundtracks, and Yes albums. There is a hymnal among the music stacked by the piano. A kitchen drawer holds containers for the aluminum pop-tops and soup-can labels we collect for our church's outreach projects. Upstairs there are Bibles, Bible storybooks, and religious novels shelved next to American Girl storybooks, Captain Underpants mysteries, and Tom Clancy novels. Two of my children have framed homemade certificates commemorating their baptisms hanging on their walls. A quilt created by the children in one of my former congregations graces one wall in the upstairs hall, its individual hand-painted squares a testimony to children's interpretations of religious life. A small, lighted ceramic church—a gift from a special aunt—serves as a nightlight in the same hallway. Bulletin boards hold an ever-changing array of religious artwork, some of it created in formal church school settings and other pieces generated at the whim of the child whose board it is. Down in the basement family room, puzzles depicting biblical stories are mixed in with ones depicting dinosaurs and Monet's garden. Some of these markers of the spiritual life would be invisible to a casual visitor, but to those of us who live in the house, they are daily reminders of our connection to God and God's desire to be known by us. To my children, religious stories, images, and songs carry at least the same fascination as nonreligious materials because they are part of the fabric of our life together as a family.

PROVIDING TOOLS FOR SPIRITUAL IMAGINATION

Children are also captivated by the things they imagine as they play. Perhaps one of the easiest ways in which we can cultivate our children's spiritual lives is by exposing them to religious stories and then providing them with the materials (props) necessary to reenact these stories in their imaginary play. An infant's woven baby carrier can become the basket that Moses lay in among the bulrushes while his big sister Miriam watched to see who would rescue him. A wooden dollhouse can become the setting for conducting religious services with a few extra pieces of furniture fashioned from cardboard or wood scraps. A water basin or table, some plastic boats, a few small figures, and a leftover piece of fruit-box netting can be transformed into disciples fishing on the Sea of Galilee. A sandbox and a collection of plastic people and animals might become the Israelites in the desert. Blankets for pitching tents encourage all kinds of journey stories to emerge, and rhythm instruments can create a beat for imitating various songs and dances that make up many religious traditions. A collection of stuffed animals can populate Noah's Ark, appear on succeeding days of a creation narrative, or replicate the image of the Peaceable Kingdom (the lion lies down with the lamb, and war is no more). Many of these items are commonplace in homes and congregations, and children are natural storytellers. All they need is access to stories and images of faith on a par with the other stories and images we provide for them, and they will incorporate the characters and narratives of religious culture into their play, just as they do with the figures and stories of the wider culture. They may even decide to include Mickey and Minnie as the pair of mice taken aboard Noah's ark to avoid the flood!

Toys that Encourage Religious Imaginary Play

Use this checklist when shopping or visiting yard sales to accumulate a collection of toys and props that can contribute to religious imaginary play. Some items can also be found among household recyclables.

Creating a Spiritual World for Children to Inhabit

- Woven infant carrier or handle-less basket large enough for a doll
- A boat large enough to hold thirteen wooden or plastic figures (and the figures to go with it)
- A plastic or foam mountain (or a volcano kit that can be remodeled as a nonerupting mountain)
- Plastic fruit netting (for water table play) or a net hammock (for larger fishing dramas)
- Pairs of animals: identical (for enacting the Noah's Ark story) or complementary (such as the Peaceable Kingdom image of the lion and the lamb)
- A sand tray or box, with people and animal figures (as well as stones and sticks from the yard)
- A small tent (or blankets) for nomadic traveling dramas
- Tambourines, recorders (or other simple pipe instruments), and streamers for singing and dancing
- Plain wooden blocks on which to draw (using permanent markers or paint) replicas of the furnishings in a house of worship
- Plastic or wooden fencing to mark off fields, sheepfolds, and temple perimeters in small-figure dramas
- A wooden dollhouse that can double for a house of worship (ancient or contemporary) or dwelling place for biblical characters
- Soft nativity set (kits available in fabric stores) and other stuffed biblical characters (or dolls redressed in biblical costumes)
- Plastic canisters, bowls, and water jugs (perhaps borrowed from the kitchen), combined with a bucket and ladle for reenacting well stories and miracle stories involving food
- Crowns and other paraphernalia for kings and queens
- Play coins and a cloth bag to hold them

REAL KIDS, REAL FAITH

Developing a Bicultural Identity

The acquisition of a bicultural identity as a member of a national culture and of a religious culture doesn't occur overnight. Developmental psychologist Erik Erikson, whose work has shaped all the literature on children's growth and behavior since the 1960s, observed that a person's identity is formed through exploration of various possibilities and an eventual commitment to certain options during adolescence or early adulthood. Providing religious images, stories, and practices for children exposes them to possibilities for a faith identity that might not otherwise be available for exploration. They can "try on" a religious perspective by imagining themselves living in the times of biblical figures. They can imitate the actions of the adult who reaches up to touch the *mezuzah* and repeat the opening words of the Shema written on its scroll: "Hear O Israel, the Lord your God, the Lord is One." They can catch a glimpse of an alternative view of the world as they piece together a picture puzzle of a saint. As they give thanks for good food and good company at the dinner table, they may wonder about the bountiful nature of God. Every time our children encounter vestiges of religious culture, their spiritual identity is clothed just a bit more in a particular garment of faith that can become a well-worn and comfortable outfit for life's journey.

Keeping Religious Culture Relevant

We must not forget, however, that religious enculturation is more than a dress-up game for children. Living a bicultural life is a family affair and a matter of importance for religious communities. When adults act as if religious education is mainly a tool for children's moral development, children quickly catch on to the irrelevance of religious culture for the grown-up world. They have no incentive for committing themselves to a particular spiritual identity in adolescence if faith is portrayed by adults as something one sheds with childhood. Their encounter with the second culture of the spiritual world becomes superficial because they do not have genuine models of adult faithful-

Creating a Spiritual World for Children to Inhabit

ness to observe and emulate. Bible storybooks read primarily to shove home a moral point for a child's own good seldom lend themselves to children's imaginary play in the same way that a story told for its drama and provocative details can do. The shallowness of rote religious gestures performed primarily for a child's edification is unmasked as the child's ability to analyze her or his culture grows. Children probe the authenticity of adult spirituality, much as they test the sincerity of parental ultimatums. If they discover that our own spiritual practices are given little explicit attention and power to shape our lives, they are likely to imitate our indifference to the religious culture. When we invite children to embrace a bicultural identity, we are committing ourselves to live within both cultures as well. The books shelved next to the Tom Clancy novels are for us, too.

Chapter 3

TELLING STORIES THAT DRAW CHILDREN INTO A LIFE OF FAITH

Literacy campaigns have become a staple of American cultural life. Public libraries sponsor summer reading programs in which children are rewarded for listening to or reading as many books as possible. Hospitals and doctors' offices in economically depressed areas give away free books provided by advocacy groups such as RIF (Reading Is Fundamental). News services supply local newspapers around the country with images of the president or first lady reading to schoolchildren. My hometown library system has a "dial-a-story" program in which children can call a special number and listen to a recording of a sports celebrity reading a popular children's book. The recordings (and stars) change weekly in an attempt to keep children calling back for more. Many schools set aside time every day or week for children to read for pleasure. We want our children to be able to use and have a strong appreciation for the power and beauty of narrative, so we invite them to explore many stories that are written for their pleasure and edification.

For over twenty years, Hebrew scripture scholar Walter Brueggemann and others have been trying to call attention to the need for a similar type of literacy campaign built around religious stories. Brueggemann understands the Bible as a book of stories that envelop the reader in the history and drama of God's activity in the world. His writings on children's spirituality counsel parents and religious leaders to see their nurturing task as helping children embrace the stories of their faith tradition so they can "affirm that this is *my* story about *me,* and it is *our* story about *us.*" Brueggemann wants children to see the connections between their own lives and the lives of biblical figures. He wants them to be able to put themselves in the story, listen to God's voice along with the characters and crowds, make decisions, and practice living the faith together with all those who have gone before.

STORY-LINKING

Anne Wimberly, whose research and teaching focus on African American Christian education, advocates a similar strategy for nurturing faith in her 1994 book *Soul Stories.* She uses the term *story-linking* to describe the way in which "persons connect components of their everyday life stories with the Christian faith story found in Scripture." Although Wimberly's work focuses primarily on the religious education of adults, it is easy to draw out the implications of this process for children and their families. Connections between personal and faith stories require that the stories of children's lives be valued by adults and that the narratives that make up the story of the religious tradition are as accessible to children as their own stories are. The unfortunate truth is that children's stories are often romanticized or devalued by busy adults who don't have much time to listen to children's chatter, and the stories of religious traditions are often told in ways that children find dull or difficult to hear. So how do we, in Brueggemann's words, "find ways of linking the big picture of [the religious story] with the immediate experiences of the child's daily life"? Brueggemann has a suggestion. He proposes that we think about nurturing children's spirituality by focusing on five activities of story-linking: receiving, hearing, celebrating, telling, and becoming.

Five Aspects of Story-Linking

Based on the work of Walter Brueggemann)

1. Children need to be *receiving* the spiritual story of love and redemption through the compassionate care of their parents and their faith community.
2. Children should be *hearing* the story of their spiritual tradition regularly in connection with the stories that make up their daily lives.
3. Children must be *celebrating* their stories of faith and personal spiritual stories through special holidays and the recognition of acts of charity and compassion.
4. Children need opportunities for *telling* spiritual stories in their own words, both to others and to God in prayer.
5. Children need ways of *becoming* "history-makers": people whose words and actions contribute to a more just and compassionate society and encourage others to do the same.

Receiving the Story

The first activity of story-linking is also a basic aspect of parenting and caregiving. It involves sharing our own experience of the sacredness of life and God's love through compassionate care for our children. In this way, children receive their religious story through the embodiment of the faithfulness of God by adults who show a similar faithfulness to them. What's at stake here is the development of basic trust, a foundational aspect of healthy human development in general and of faith formation in particular. When children experience that their needs will be met consistently and lovingly by the people around them, they are better able to imagine a consistent and loving God who cares for them as well. And because very young children associate

Telling Stories That Draw Children into a Life of Faith

their caregivers with God (seeing in them the same attributes of tremendous power, knowledge, and ability to shape the world that human beings often ascribe to God), the influence of early human relationships communicates much about how God's love is present (or not) in the world of the child.

Religious communities share with parents the responsibility to help children receive the faith story through godly human actions. Many congregations believe that this responsibility can be met by hiring a high-quality child-care provider to staff their nursery during religious services. This approach can certainly contribute to cultivating trust, in the general sense that Erik Erikson (a developmental psychologist whose work has shaped much of our contemporary understanding about early childhood) meant when he spoke of the importance of a child learning that the world is reliable and will dependably meet one's needs. It does not, however, communicate the more particular characteristics of hospitality and compassion that can and should mark the culture of a religious community. For children to receive their own religious story in its fullest embodiment, parents and caregivers need to provide a fullness of care that mimics the faithful relationships described in the narratives of their tradition's sacred texts. These texts often portray a lavishness of hospitality and a measure of compassion that doesn't match our usual ways of incorporating children into an adult-oriented world.

Acts of Hospitality   Consider, for instance, the story of how Rebekah was selected to be the wife of Isaac—a story that is common to Judaism, Christianity, and Islam. Abraham (Isaac's father and patriarch of all three faith traditions) sends a servant back to his homeland to find a woman willing to travel to Canaan and wed Abraham's son. The servant, concerned that no woman will want to leave her home to marry a man living in a different culture, decides that it will take more than gifts of jewelry and fine clothing to make this match. Arriving back in the old country at just about the time young women would gather at the village well to draw water for their households, the servant prays for God's guidance. He says, "Let the girl to whom I shall say, 'Please offer your jar that I may drink,' and who shall say, 'Drink, and I will water your camels'—let her be the one whom you have appointed for your servant Isaac. By this I shall know that you have shown steadfast love to my master" (Genesis 24:14). The servant's test is based on a sign of abundant hospitality; Rebekah, the girl who not only offers the minimal hospitality of a drink of water to the servant but extends that hospitality to include caring for the servant's animals, signifies God's steadfast love by her actions.

How might parents and religious communities practice Rebekah's kind of abundant hospitality with children? If we imagine that providing for children's basic need for security and predictability is akin to providing a drink to slake the servant's thirst, then our challenge is to identify the "camels"—the additional needs of children—that we can tend to as well. Rebekah chose to welcome the servant and all his "baggage." What baggage do our children bring with them that we might welcome rather than simply endure?

Young children are messy, demanding creatures. They desire large doses of close human contact; they may not have learned to use a toilet; they often cry at the most inopportune times, and they generate an amazing amount of laundry. Our culture has invented myriad ways to accommodate an adult preference for activities other than child care that permit us to avoid or delay dealing with common childhood needs. The infant car seat that conveniently doubles as a carrier also acts as a barrier to direct human contact. And the mechanical swing that soothes fussy babies in the church nursery communicates that people receive comfort from things rather than from other people. The distaste with which we change diapers and wipe up spittle, the haste with which we hurry a preschooler who's examining a bug on the sidewalk, the videos we pop into the VCR to keep a child occupied while we do housework or chat with a friend—all of these are the sometimes-appropriate responses to life with children that have become the norm of adult-child interactions.

Congregations have even become adept at labeling the practice of excluding children from worship (the primary work of a religious community) as a form of age-appropriate hospitality, without recognizing that "separate-but-equal" doesn't work any better in congregational

45

life than it did as a racist practice in the 1950s and 1960s. The lack of physical control, tendency toward emotional outbursts, different ways of attending to external stimuli, and alternative ways of comprehending information that constitute our children's baggage in an adult world seldom elicit a Rebekah-like response of abundant hospitality in us. For children to receive the story of God's abundant love for them, then, we must change our ways of being present to and with children at home and in communities of faith.

The Concept of Godparenting   One way to make such change is to embrace the notion of godparenting as an intentional practice of relating with children. Many Christian traditions that baptize infants encourage parents to select one or two other adults who will

Gauging Our Hospitality to Children

Very few parents set out to be intentionally inhospitable to their own children. Instead, we get caught up in the pronouncements made by baby product manufacturers that various devices are necessary for good parenting, without always noticing what may be lost in the process of using the products. Or we have jobs and volunteer responsibilities that expand to fill so much time that we can't imagine any other pace but rushing. Our children enjoy videos and beg to see their favorites over and over again, and our desire to get just one more task accomplished or sneak a little down time with a book inclines us to give in to their demands. So how do we know if we're making good decisions that welcome children as they are and still acknowledge our own legitimate needs? Perhaps reflecting on the following questions periodically can help us define and practice the right mix of household hospitality for our children and ourselves.

intentionally assist them in helping their child learn what it means to have a relationship with God. What I am proposing is that we take this idea of naming a few godparents per child and extend it to include the perspective that all adults are godparents of all the world's children. In this sense, we recognize that our primary role as parents and as faith communities in relation to children is to care for children in the manner God would care for them. Elaine Ramshaw, in *The Godparent Book,* puts it this way: "When you make God's love real to a child by your own deep appreciation of and delight in and patience with the child, you are communicating to him or her what it means to be God's beloved." Similarly, when we advocate for the well-being of children within and outside our immediate community who are hungry, abused, orphaned, and suffering, we embody

- How often have I communicated to my child today that his or her body is a wonderful and amazing creation?
- In what ways have I modeled good self-care to my child by the way I honor my own body's needs?
- In what ways has my child felt close to the other members of our family today? When have I felt especially close to my child today?
- In what ways have I made space for my child to tell me about the things that interest him or her? Based on observing me, what would my child say are the most important things in my life?

Sometimes such introspection can lead to feelings of guilt or unrealistic expectations for future practices. Guilt is only helpful if it motivates us to make realistic changes that acknowledge the limits of human effort and the value of learning from our mistakes. Let these questions be guides, not judges, as you set out to be an intentionally child- and parent-friendly home.

Telling Stories That Draw Children into a Life of Faith

God's love for the poor and disenfranchised. We become parents-like-God, offering to children the experience of godly love so that they might receive the story as their birthright.

Ideas for Godparenting Any Child

Elaine Ramshaw offers numerous ideas for fostering relationships with children that embody God's love and justice. Try these ideas, reproduced from *The Godparent Book,* as a way of helping children "receive the story." Remember, any adult—even an actual parent—can adopt godparent behavior.

- Listen to your godchild, and take what she says as seriously as you would if she were a grown-up friend. Look at her when she talks, let her finish her sentences, make comments that repeat part of what she said so she knows you're really listening.
- Look for things to appreciate in your godchild, and tell him what you see. Praise him when he's helpful, kind, brave, creative. If everybody complains about some quality of his, try to find a way to recast it in a more positive light. Never compare him to his brothers or sisters.
- Tell stories about your own childhood, not "when I was your age" stories that are really disguised lectures but stories about experiences that might connect to things the child is going through. What scared you, excited you, disappointed you, angered you, or interested you when you were your godchild's age? Do the two of you have experiences in common—music lessons, sports, studies, great or horrible teachers, loyal or treacherous friends—that you can compare feelings about?

REAL KIDS, REAL FAITH

Four Kinds of Faith Storybooks

1. Stories that try to remain close to biblical translations
2. Stories that employ *midrash,* a Jewish term meaning a story about a biblical story
3. Stories that link a human story (or the reader) to a biblical story or theme
4. Stories that "incarnate" (render in a human likeness) biblical principles

All four kinds of books contribute to children's exploration of spirituality and development of spiritual identity. A home or faith community library might strive to have some of each type so that children and their adult caregivers can hear the spiritual story through a broad spectrum of approaches, characters, and contexts.

Hearing the Story

The second activity of story-linking picks up the commonplace understanding of what it means to tell children stories: adults need to tell children religious narratives so that children are "hearing the story" of God's love as it has been told throughout the ages. Through reading, storytelling, looking at pictures, preaching, teaching, play-acting, and singing, parents and faith communities can invite children to hear the stories of their tradition.

The highly popular *Veggie Tales* videos and children's Bible storybooks are resources many adults turn to for help in communicating the same stories they may remember from their childhood. Although these resources can be problematic in the ways they portray story characters (I once listened to a two-year-old *Veggie Tales* veteran insist to his four-year-old friend that God is a tomato—confusing God with the central *Veggie Tales* character, Bob, who *is* a tomato), they are also creative attempts to engage children imaginatively in the stories of their religious culture. If we as adults recognize that stories can be told in many ways, we can provide a variety of storybooks, videos, and other resources from which our children may hear the story.

Close Readings   I've noticed that books with spiritual themes fall primarily into four categories. First, there are stories that try to remain close to the sacred scriptures of their religious tradition; these are called close readings. This category includes Bible storybooks and religious holiday books that use the words of the tradition's scriptures as their texts. When children read these stories or when adults read them aloud to children, they hear the stories of their religious culture told in the traditional language of the culture. They become acquainted with the words that are familiar to others around the world who speak their religious language in the same tongue. If they participate in different communities of faith throughout their childhood or adult lives, these shared words will help connect their various experiences to a common narrative.

Sometimes religious communities create books of this sort specifically to pass on oral stories of their tradition to their children. The Jataka Tales, which are stories that Buddhists believe the Buddha told more than two thousand years ago, have been retold for contemporary children in a series of paperbacks created by Dharma Publishing. Adapted from the Buddha's account of his previous lives, books such as *The Rabbit Who Overcame Fear* convey the principles of Buddhism through some of the stories that are at the heart of the tradition's teachings. When children of any tradition read these stories, they learn more about Buddhism and what it means for its adherents—an important discovery, given the religious diversity of the typical school classroom in the twenty-first century.

Adults often worry about the appropriateness of some religious stories for young children. Toddlers and preschoolers, however, do not experience the moral tension so apparent to an adult reader. Their attention is caught instead by the simple images that a story presents:

a mother and father with a baby, a man swallowed by a big fish, a woman working in a field. They don't ask about the fairness of Jesus being born in a stable rather than a hospital, question Jonah's motives in refusing and then going to Ninevah, or pick up on the sexual innuendo in Ruth's interactions with her cousin Laban as she gleans wheat in his fields. They have neither the experience nor the cognitive capability to factor these issues into their engagement with the story. Instead, they focus on who and what, leaving the other details for future encounters.

Providing children with books that follow the scriptures closely is crucial because otherwise they will not recognize that the religious stories they are hearing are the same stories their parents and the rest of their religious community are hearing. Books with close readings help children recognize that religious stories are meant to be shared across generations. They invite children to imagine living with the guidance of a good story for a lifetime, rather than loving it for a while and then casting it aside as "too babyish" or simple to be meaningful later on. They also encourage us to wonder aloud with our children about the ways in which people across time and space have responded to the words we are now reading together.

Stories About the Tradition's Stories   The second type of spiritual story is one that employs the Jewish practice of telling midrash, or a story *about* a biblical story. Here the author borrows an interesting character or detail from the scriptures and spins a provocative tale around that character or detail in a way that calls attention to an important idea or spiritual principle. The goal of the story is not to explain the biblical text; rather, the author hopes that the midrash will help the reader understand the meaning of the original story a little bit better by hearing a part of it from a different perspective. Judaism calls those who write such stories *darshanim,* and the Jewish tradition contains many collections of midrashim.

One of my favorite contemporary *darshanim* is Marc Gellman, a rabbi and father of two, who has written two collections of midrashim for children. In *Does God Have a Big Toe?* the title story is about the Tower of Babel narrative in Genesis 11:1–9. The biblical text tells the

Telling Stories That Draw Children into a Life of Faith

reader that at one time everyone on earth spoke the same language. This homogeneous community decided to build a tower reaching up into the heavens so that they might climb up and join God as gods themselves. When God saw what they were doing, God decided to introduce a diversity of languages so that the people could no longer understand one another. Without the ability to communicate, they would not be able to complete the deed. Gellman retells the story by imagining an inquisitive child as the source of the community's decision to build the tower. The child, Arinna, goes to her mother and asks, "Mommy, I have a big toe, and you have a big toe, and Daddy has a big toe. Does God have a big toe too?" When her mother is too busy to answer her question, she tries her father, then her grandfather and her grandfather's friend. The grandfather's friend, Fred, takes the question to the king, who proclaims, "You, the people of Babel, will build a tower up to the sky so that I, your king, can stand on top of this tower and look at God's foot. Then I will tell you if God has a big toe." God, seeing all the activity around the tower, becomes concerned that no one is doing their usual work of growing food and providing supplies for the life of the community. Recognizing that the community cannot survive without people caring for its life together, God decides something must be done. God makes it impossible for the tower workers to understand one another, and the people of the world community decide to separate according to who can understand whom and create new communities throughout the earth.

Another teller of stories about stories in the Bible is Sandy Sasso, whose popular children's books are best-sellers. In *A Prayer for the Earth: The Story of Naamah, Noah's Wife,* Sasso invites children to imagine what the biblically nameless wife of Noah was doing while her husband gathered the animals into the ark. God gives Naamah, whose name comes from the Jewish word for "pleasing," the task of gathering seeds from all the earth's plants so that gardens, forests, and fields can be replanted after the flood. She wasn't allowed to leave any seeds out, not even the dandelions. Sasso writes,

> Naamah walked into the fields right past the dandelions, pretending not to notice their feathery yellow heads

sprouting over the grass. "Naamah," called God, "gather seeds of *every* living plant!" And Naamah knew that God meant the dandelions too. Reluctantly, she placed their seeds in her pockets with all the others. Because Naamah had ignored them, God made certain that dandelions would cover the earth.

Through such humorous observations, Sasso helps children imagine why their world is populated with so many and such diverse plants and provides a model for the appreciation and loving care of all God's creation in the person of Naamah.

It is not only Jewish authors who tell midrash. Avril Rowlands, a British television producer and Christian, has written a series of books about biblical stories from the perspective of the animals who are present (or imagined to be present) at certain significant events. Her first book, *Tales from the Ark,* recounts the story of Noah and the flood through the eyes of thirteen different animals, from a termite to an elephant. When it comes time for the animals to leave the ark, Rowland imagines that several of the animals are afraid to leave because they don't know if they can survive in the new world. After much discussion, they agree to form a "United League of Animals" pledged to look after one another, but they cannot agree on who should lead the society. The mouse suggests that Noah should be the head. Noah asks God whether it is right that he should take on such a huge responsibility. God replies, "I give all the creatures of the world into your hands. Look after them well." This last tale in the book invites children to think about what it means to care for God's creatures.

Another Christian writer, Martha Hickman, tells a story about the story of creation in *And God Created Squash: How the World Began.* She imagines God's delight in creating things. The title of the book comes from her description of what happened after God created the first squash.

"I like that name," God said. "I think I'll use it again. Acorn squash. Butternut squash. Even zucchini squash. I might have a game and call it squash. Or put my hand on something and press down hard and call that squash," God said.

Like Sasso, she employs humor to encourage children to see the connections between God's creation of the world and the world in which they live.

Hearing stories about the tradition's stories prompts children to wonder about the background and context of those stories and to ask themselves how those details affect their understanding of the stories. It picks up on a common school-teacher practice of asking children to imagine a different ending to a story or to fill in the gaps in a story's details so that the reason for the given outcome is clearer. When we read this type of story with our children in conjunction with books that provide close readings of our tradition's stories, we are teaching our children to pay attention to what is and isn't said in a story and how those details may or may not support certain interpretations. We are also helping them see that there is generally more than one way of interpreting a story and imagining oneself living faithfully in response to it. In short, we are firing up their imaginations, while still providing some boundaries (in the guise of what the original story does tell us) within which to let their ideas develop.

Books Linking Tradition and Contemporary Life   Children can also hear the story through books that explicitly take some aspect or issue of contemporary life and relate that concern to scripture or the practices of the religious tradition. Sometimes this linkage takes the form of telling a story to explain religious customs, such as those related to the Jewish holidays or Christian sacraments. Popular author Tomie dePaola has written several books that retell holiday legends or the stories of saints revered in his Catholic tradition. Other times, such books compare life in a child's world with the life of religious persons in a different era. Peter Graystone and Jacqui Thomas begin their book *If I Had Lived in Jesus' Time* with the words, "Last night I had a dream. I dreamed that I was alive hundreds of years ago—when Jesus was growing up in Nazareth." The rest of the story walks the reader through a typical day in the life of a child in the twenty-first century and in the first century C.E. with simple text such as: "Today it is my turn to look after the animals. They are in a naughty mood. Do you have any animals in your home?" The child sees illustrations of children caring for animals in both eras, and the text invites the reader to put himself or herself in the story with the characters.

One of the most famous books linking modern childhood and religious concerns is Judy Blume's classic, *Are You There God? It's Me, Margaret.* The central character, almost-twelve-year-old Margaret, has a lot of questions about life in general and what it means to be religious in particular. Her father, who is Jewish, and her mother, who was raised in a Christian home, consider themselves nonreligious and want their only child to wait until she is an adult to decide what religion, if any, she will be. Her paternal grandmother, who is a strong influence in Margaret's life, fervently hopes Margaret will decide to be Jewish but tries not to interfere with the parents' wish to raise their child without any particular tradition. Unbeknownst to all of them, Margaret has regular conversations with God about her questions, worries, and desires. For her sixth-grade project, she decides to explore Judaism and Christianity. She plans to visit services at her grandmother's temple and at several churches, as well as read about both religions. After her first visit to temple on Rosh Hashanah (the Jewish New Year), Margaret has a conversation with God.

> Are you there God? It's me, Margaret. I'm really on my way now. By the end of the school year I'll know all there is to know about religion. And before I start junior high I'll know which one I am. Then I'll be able to join the Y[MCA] or the [Jewish Community] Center like everybody else.

Blume weaves Margaret's religious concerns and her emotional and social concerns together in this way throughout the book, providing older elementary and middle school children (especially girls) with a character who thinks and asks questions similar to their own.

Mark Gellman and Sandy Sasso have written books that fall into this third category as well. Gellman has teamed up with Thomas

Telling Stories That Draw Children into a Life of Faith

Hartman, a Catholic priest, to help children and the adults who care for them answer common questions about God and spirituality. In *Where Does God Live?,* the team considers such questions as, "When my pet hamster Elmo died, did he go to heaven?" and "Is it okay to get angry at God?" In *How Do You Spell God?,* they help families think about the differences and similarities among the world's major religious traditions. There are chapters on beliefs about death, religious schism, and "what question does each religion want to answer the most?" as well as the standard concerns about religious holidays, scriptures, and worship practices. Sasso's books, *God's Paintbrush* and *God in Between,* draw children into conversations about what God is like and where God can be found, the former with direct questions and the latter through the telling of a modern fable.

Both parents and children find books that link tradition and contemporary life helpful because it is difficult sometimes to understand how the Bible, which was written thousands of years ago, could still be relevant today. Our families may know little about biblical times and the issues that affected the people and communities of those eras. What we do know is that so many of the things that make up our daily existence didn't exist fifty or a hundred years ago, let alone way back in the times of Adam and Eve or Jesus. Books that help us see the ways in which the issues of our lives are similar to those faced by biblical people and the timelessness of community concerns like justice, fairness, and dealing with strangers lend credence to the idea that the Bible can be a valuable contemporary guide for living. Discovering that the scriptures may not mention electronic media (television, computers, CD players) directly and yet have much to say about avoiding stereotypes (an issue in television commercials and sitcoms) and the fair use of resources (pertinent to the question of downloading music clips and burning pirated CDs) opens our children's eyes to how their tradition really does speak to their world. It is crucial, however, that we read this type of book alongside the Bible and books that provide close readings of the scriptures. Otherwise, children may not realize that they can go directly to the source of this information and draw their own conclusions rather than rely solely on someone else's interpretation.

Stories Exemplifying Spiritual Principles   The fourth type of story is one that takes a spiritual principle like "hospitality" or "compassion" and illustrates it through the life and actions of a fictitious character. I call these incarnational stories because they show what the divine looks like in human form. They help children see how the character lives out his or her spiritual commitments, which encourages them to imagine themselves living in similar ways. Sometimes the connection to a particular religious tradition is explicit in the text, and sometimes the child must intuit the connection based on their previous encounter with the spiritual principle in a religious community. Stories with more explicit connections provide the link between particular beliefs and practices that children are just learning to notice and understand. They supply the language and context for making religious meaning of the character's actions. Intuitive incarnational stories require children to create this link for themselves. Children who have had little enculturation in a religious tradition may sense significance in these stories, but they are less likely to interpret the story as an expression of spiritual commitment. Rather, they will use alternative frameworks for meaning, such as their school's code of conduct, their family rules, or the moral norms they observe in the media.

Two examples of explicitly religious incarnational stories are Patricia Polacco's *Chicken Sunday* and Jan Karon's *Miss Fannie's Hat.* A popular children's author, Polacco spins a tale of three children who are determined to buy their "gramma," Miss Eula, a special hat for Easter Sunday service. Two of the children are Miss Eula's biological grandchildren; the third is a neighbor girl who "adopted" Miss Eula as part of her own family after her own grandmother died. All three children regularly accompany Miss Eula to Sunday services at the Baptist church, then eat fried chicken for lunch with her afterward. When Miss Eula admires a beautiful hat in the window of Mr. Kodinski's shop, the children decide they must overcome their fear of the "strange old man" in order to surprise her with the hat. After a dismal first attempt, in which Mr. Kodinski mistakenly accuses them of throwing eggs at his shop door, the children decide to decorate Easter eggs as a peace offering for Mr. Kodinski. Little do they realize that the Ukrainian *pysanky* (folk art) decorations they have chosen will

Telling Stories That Draw Children into a Life of Faith

touch the Russian storekeeper's heart more deeply than they could ever imagine. The hat is eventually obtained and, along with it, the shopkeeper's proclamation that the children "are very good children, such good children!" An astute adult or older child realizes from a few details in the story that Mr. Kodinski's apparent strangeness is related to his memories of the Holocaust as a Russian Jew. His graciousness in receiving the Easter eggs, which are not of his religious tradition yet remind him of home, complements the children's sincerity in reaching out to him with compassion, despite their fears and the misunderstanding about their behavior. Miss Eula's joyous receipt of her gift is underscored by her wearing the hat while she sings the solo in the Easter choir and in the way she laughs "from a deep, holy place inside." The book portrays an active spirituality that comes from participation in religious community and spiritual commitments to compassion, hospitality, and joy for all people, even those outside one's intimate circle.

Miss Fannie's Hat chronicles the decision of a beloved grandmother figure who has been asked to donate one of her signature Sunday hats for the church auction. Each hat has tremendous sentimental value, and Miss Fannie struggles with her desire to keep them all for herself. Finally, as she repeats her favorite Bible verse to herself ("With God, all things are possible"), she wraps up her favorite Easter hat with the hope that it will raise a lot of money for patching the church roof or repairing the organ. The hat does indeed sell for a lot of money. Everyone adores Miss Fannie's hats, especially the Easter hat with all its pink roses, and Miss Fannie is both happy and sad. What will she wear on Easter Sunday now that her hat is gone? She arrives at the church Easter morning hatless, only to discover that pink roses have been planted all around the building. The church is "wearing" her hat! Karon, who is best known for her Mitford novels for adults, offers children a glimpse into the practices of spiritual discernment and hospitality in the life and actions of an endearing character.

Magical Hands, by Marjorie Barker, and *An Angel for Solomon Singer,* by Newbery medalist Cynthia Rylant, convey incarnate spiritual principles more subtly. Barker's story involves four shopkeepers who are best friends. Over lunch one day, one of them says wistfully that he wishes there was a magical tool to do his work on his birthday so he could take it easy instead of tending to business all day. Another member of the group, William, plays the conversation over in his head later. Barker writes, "He held out his two strong, rough hands. Perhaps there were no magical tools to help them, but he had all that he needed to make a birthday wish come true for each of his three friends." William rises early on his friends' birthdays and does their chores for them: stacking Vincent's fruit in his stalls, washing Philip's general store windows, and kneading Adrian's dough. He then tries to hide his delight as each friend puzzles happily over the "magic" that has been wrought. William assumes that his own birthday will be ordinary, since he has kept his secret so well. But when he arises on that morning, all his wood has been chopped and his table has been set with warm bread from Adrian's bakery and some of Vincent's strawberries in a bowl from Philip's store. Bowing his head, he closes his eyes and sits quietly a moment. "When he opened his eyes, they were shining. It is a wonderful thing, he thought, to have magical hands."

Rylant's central character is Solomon Singer. She describes him this way: "Solomon Singer was lonely and had no one to love and not even a place to love, and this was hard for him." One day, he discovers a restaurant called The Westway Café that has the motto, "where all your dreams come true." Solomon Singer returns to the restaurant night after night, and as he orders dinner from the kindly waiter who always bids him welcome, he imagines himself ordering up all the comforts he wishes he had in a place to live: a balcony, a fireplace, a porch swing, a picture window, a pet. After a time, he realizes that The Westway Café has become the very place he longs for, not because it has the exact amenities he's been dreaming about but because there he feels welcome and no longer lonely. The waiter, whom Rylant names "Angel," becomes for Solomon Singer the embodiment and the model of hospitality and community he so desperately needs. Soon Solomon Singer has become a part of the smiling welcome that strangers receive when they happen upon The Westway Café for the first time. Children see in this story the way in which one person's actions can transform the life of another person and then multiply through the formation of an intentionally hospitable community.

Telling Stories That Draw Children into a Life of Faith

Children's Own Stories   The last two kinds of storybooks are especially helpful in drawing forth elements of children's own stories in relation to the stories of their tradition. Recall that Brueggemann understands the spiritual life as the connecting of one's own story with the stories of one's religious tradition in ways that create personal and communal identification with an integrated story formed from the connections. Such a merger cannot occur if children do not hear their own lives told alongside and in conversation with traditional stories. In books that do not supply easy entry points into children's personal stories, adults, reading aloud with children, can interject references to the child's world along the way or strike up a conversation about possible connections afterward.

Celebrating the Story

Brueggemann moves from advocating that children receive and hear their traditions' stories to urging that we offer children opportunities to celebrate the integrated story formed through their personal engagement with their faith communities' stories. He notes that such celebrations "enrich our children with a very special historical imagination" that expands their sense of community across time and space. Even when children do not understand the logic that shapes a particular event, they intuit the meaning of the celebration by processing the sounds, sights, smells, rhythms, and emotions of the experience.

Religious Celebrations   Celebrations often take the form of rituals related to religious holidays: eating latkes and applesauce for Hanukkah or rising early for an Easter sunrise service, for example. Weekly observances of Shabbat and corporate worship are also celebrations, as are special occasions such as baptism, a *bris* (the ritual circumcision of Jewish boys), first communion, confirmation (in which youth confirm the claims of their baptism as infants), and funerals. All of these are events and rituals that people have participated in for thousands of years and numerous generations. When our children participate in them as well, they become actors in a vast historical and multicultural drama—characters in a story that had its begin-

REAL KIDS, REAL FAITH

ning long before they were born, is enacted around the world today, and will continue to be told long after they die.

Religious and Community Celebrations   The last item (funerals) may seem an odd item to include in a list of celebrations. But if we consider the ways in which funerals and memorial services commemorate the life of the deceased *and* the community's beliefs about the afterlife, the celebratory nature of the event is more apparent. In fact, the interweaving of personal and traditional stories that marks a well-designed funeral provides a model for how we might help children celebrate this interweaving in the more ordinary moments of their lives.

It is a simple model that surrounds words of remembrance about a person's personal life story with the words of the faith tradition's story through hymns, scripture readings, proclamations, prayers, and blessings. We can translate this model into our children's everyday lives by watching for opportunities to surround their personal activities with references to the spiritual dimensions of their story. We can liken children's decisions to stand up for themselves or for what is right by recalling the biblical story of the boy David, who took on the boastful and bullying Goliath (1 Samuel 17) or the testimonies of Martin Luther King Jr. and Rosa Parks, whose faithfulness led them to engage in civil disobedience. We can wonder together about the beauty and complexity of God's creation when our little ones stop to watch a line of ants carry bits of leaf across the sidewalk. We can recall the story of Dorcas, an early Christian woman who provided food and clothing to the needy (Acts 9:36–42), as we help our preteens sort through their outgrown clothing for items to donate. On a more daily basis, we can offer thanks for our food at meals and for God's presence with us throughout the day at bedtime.

Everyday Celebration   Discover more traditional stories to celebrate alongside a child's activities by reading a Bible storybook or other collection of stories representing the family's tradition. One doesn't have to be a religious scholar to celebrate the intertwining of tradition and personal life, but sometimes one does need to be a detective!

Telling Stories That Draw Children into a Life of Faith

In addition to investigating communal faith stories, we have to be attentive to our children's lives so that we notice moments when celebrations of the linkage between their lives and their tradition's beliefs and practices are appropriate. Think of this as watching for the teachable moment that preschool teachers and public school educators espouse. There are times when our children's minds and

Spiritual Celebrations for Ordinary Events

There are many aspects of daily life and our regular family routines that lend themselves to connections with our stories of faith, but designing small celebrations that draw attention to this congruence takes forethought and practice. With the following list of twenty ordinary events in mind, read through a family story Bible (my favorite is Ralph Milton's *The Family Story Bible*), looking for biblical stories that resonate with one event or another. Then come up with a ritual or action that might celebrate the link between the faith story you've found and the ordinary life event with which you've paired it. (Note the examples following the first two items on the list.) Try out your celebrations with your children, revising them as experience teaches you how better to acknowledge the sacredness of ordinary experiences.

Ordinary Experiences and Events
- Preparing a meal (Pair with the story of Abraham and Sarah's special visitors in Genesis 18, and plan to share dreams for the future while the family dines. Or pair with the story of Jesus' conversation with Martha in Luke 10:38–42, and have each person name a food they like that is good for them and something else that one doesn't eat but helps one be spiritually healthy.)

hearts are wondering how to make meaning of what they see and do; when we evoke our tradition's stories at those times, we help our children celebrate their participation in that ongoing saga. And when we take care to avoid contrived object lessons and let our children's actual lives show us and them the way to make moral connections, everyone feels like celebrating.

- Cleaning house (For my children, cleaning their rooms is often initiated because they can't find something they've misplaced. This situation brings to mind the story of the woman in Luke 15:8–10 who sweeps her entire house looking for a lost coin in one of Jesus' parables about God's love for all people.)
- Beginning of the work or school week
- Taking a family vacation away from home
- Driving or riding across town
- Making a trip to the grocery store
- Buying new clothes
- Doing the laundry
- Doing yard work
- Washing the dishes
- Watching television
- Taking a walk
- Paying the bills or managing an allowance
- Setting the table
- Listening to the radio
- Looking at vacation photos
- Making a to-do list
- Eating breakfast
- Talking to a telemarketer
- Talking with a neighbor

Telling Stories That Draw Children into a Life of Faith

Telling the Story

Brueggemann's fourth aspect of story-linking focuses on children's storytelling. For a story to become a part of a child's personal understanding of the world, she needs to put that story in her own words. We've all heard children repeat words they've overheard adults use without really comprehending what they are saying. Children may do the same thing with religious stories when they first hear them. If they are going to move beyond rote memorization of a particular set of words to meaningful articulations, we have to let them talk about the stories they hear and try out their own versions.

In Their Own Words　Remember the two-year-old I mentioned earlier, who was convinced God is a tomato after he watched a *Veggie Tales* video? He was telling the story as he understood it. His version gives us insight into how he has constructed personal meaning out of what he has heard. Without other visual images or descriptions of God to compete with the vegetables he saw on his television screen, and given his typical toddler propensity to confuse like-sounding words, he picked up the references to Bob (the tomato) and God (who isn't depicted visually), conflated them, and associated them with the image provided for Bob. It may be inaccurate, but it makes sense to him. Given time and exposure to other possible ways of imagining God outside the *Veggie Tales* realm, he will tell his story of who God is differently.

Children put stories in their own words by linking them to their own experiences or understandings of social life. An eight-year-old in one of my church school classes tied her experience of family and public school discipline to the story of Jesus' crucifixion and explained to the rest of the class that Jesus died because people didn't use their words. She said that people got so angry they wouldn't talk about things and that the whole situation would have been different if the people who were mad had just taken a time out. By inviting her to share her version of the story (a version her peers vigorously supported), I provided a space for her to make the story her story as well as mine. As the other children listened to her words and then added their thoughts, they continued the storytelling process.

Using Their Imagination   When we read a traditional story with children, we can ask them to tell the story back to us later in the day or week. We can play a game in which we wonder together what some biblical character would look, sound, and act like if he or she lived in our neighborhood. We might encourage our children to catch us living faithfully, according to the beliefs and practices of our tradition, and identify which religious person our actions seem to emulate. We can invite older children and teens to explore what their religious tradition has to say to them about their issues and concerns and listen as they tell us what they're thinking about the connections.

School teachers frequently ask children to illustrate stories as a means of retelling them because drawing a picture helps children visually depict the characters and events about which they have heard. We can invite our children to create a mural for their bedroom or playroom wall that includes scenes from their favorite Bible stories. Older children might create comic strip renditions of stories or trading cards containing an image and a synopsis of the noteworthy facts (in their estimation) about various biblical characters. One of my younger children's favorite activities was to create a game (in the style of either Monopoly or The Game of Life) using places or characters from the Bible. (The children got this idea from all the variations on Monopoly, such as Cat-opoly and Indiana-opoly, they had seen in stores.) Washable window paints or markers turn glass surfaces into storyboards on which children can tell the stories of their tradition to the neighborhood, especially around religious holidays, then wash one set away and begin again.

Much of our children's development as storytellers is dependent on our own comfort level with religious conversation. If we are worried about what the neighbors will think if they see a child's rendition of Joseph and his coat of many colors on our sliding-glass door, then we are unlikely to encourage that avenue of storytelling. If that is the only avenue with which we're uncomfortable, there will be plenty of other opportunities for our children to explore. But if, in our discomfort, we communicate to our children that religious storytelling belongs only within the confines of church school or parent-initiated

Telling Stories That Draw Children into a Life of Faith

private conversations, our children are likely to abandon their attempts to articulate the religious stories they have heard. The desire to please one's parents and avoid parental displeasure is strong in children, and they will not continue to initiate talk about topics they believe make their parents unhappy. So put the windows off-limits if you must, but invite other means of storytelling on a regular basis.

Becoming the Story

The fifth aspect of story-linking takes storytelling a step farther into story-living. As the popular saying goes, "If you're gonna talk the talk, you gotta walk the walk." Becoming the story is about walking the walk in such a "full of faith" way that other people's lives are transformed by the encounter. These may be small transformations, like the smile of joy generated in response to a child's generous presentation of a dandelion "for you, Mommy." Or the transformation may be larger, as in cases where children's idealistic crusades to provide enough teddy bears for all those with cancer or sufficient blankets for all the homeless in their city lead adults and their organizations to join in the effort.

The recent revival of nineteenth-century pastor Charles Sheldon's question, "What would Jesus do?" in the "WWJD" trinkets available for sale in Christian bookstores is an attempt to help children (and adults) embody Christian beliefs and practices. Sheldon's idea, laid out in his book, *In His Steps,* was that people would pledge to make no decision in their lives nor take any significant action without asking themselves what Jesus would do in their place. Since 1896, more than six million copies have been in circulation, posing this challenge to generation after generation of Christians. The Jataka Tales series I described earlier plays a similar role in the Buddhist tradition. We could also couch this question in terms of any of the faithful people described in scripture: What would Abraham (whose faith was reckoned as righteousness) do? What would Miriam (who led the Israelites in praising God after their escape from Egypt) do? By doing so, we let the stories about our religious forebears become our guides.

Children (and adults) who are "becoming the story" by living faithfully are learning what it means to engage in a way of life that links spiritual awareness to daily practice. All persons, young and old, need ways of reminding themselves that the spiritual life must be lived actively as well as contemplatively. When we help children practice the same kind of abundant hospitality we offered them as a means of experiencing the story of their tradition, we invite them to participate in a new cycle of story-linking.

STORY-LINKING AND COMPASSION

When we offer children stories as a means of linking the seemingly abstract language of beliefs and values to the immediate experiences of their daily lives, we are providing space for compassion to develop and flourish. All the major religious traditions uphold care and concern for others as a central tenet. Thus the languages and practices of faith traditions can provide children with an interpretive basis for sustainable and intentional identity as a compassionate person. But these languages and practices simultaneously push us to greater spiritual awareness and call us to account for our own embodiment of compassion. As adults, we cannot simply wonder whether we have lost touch with that which might nurture and sustain our living. We must actively reconnect ourselves with the narratives and practices on which we depend for meaningful life and examine our conscience for ways we have both succeeded and failed to embody compassion. In this way, we become partners with our children in the spiritual process of story-linking, and along the way we grow together in compassion for one another and the world.

Telling Stories That Draw Children into a Life of Faith

Chapter 4

HELPING CHILDREN NAME GOD'S PRESENCE IN THEIR LIVES

❧✦❧

We read stories to children not simply because we want to acquaint them with the characters and plots but because hearing us speak helps them acquire language. Our words train their ear for the cadences of speech, expose them to the vocabulary of our tongue and dialect, and familiarize them with the conventions of narrative. Without our speech surrounding them, children would have difficulty learning to speak, for they would have no models for how to organize sounds into words, words into sentences, and sentences into meaningful stories of their own.

Families that speak more than one language in the home face a double challenge, for their children need exposure to two different styles of speech, two vocabularies, and two sets of narrative conventions. Competence in either language comes more slowly, as children sort out which sounds and what order belong to each language. Yet children who learn two languages from a young age move between those two languages much more easily and fluently than do adults who attempt to acquire a second language later in life. A three-year-old exposed to bilingualism since birth will be as competent in either language as another preschooler raised to speak only one language.

Nurturing the spiritual lives of children requires us to encourage a bilingualism of a similar sort. Religious traditions have their own vocabulary—their own narrative conventions that can seem mysterious or remote to those unfamiliar with the language. Both children and adults need exposure to the grammar of the religious life so that they can understand and participate in religious conversation. If parents are already fluent in the language of the family's tradition and speak that language at home, then children easily adopt it as a second tongue. But if, as is more common among contemporary households, parents also need to become bilingual, then the task requires more effort and additional resources.

A few blocks from my house there is an international school where children can study in two languages simultaneously. Most of the children who attend the school speak only English when they enter. But through immersion in and study of a second language, they gradually learn to communicate in either Spanish or French; in addition, they gain a more mature use of English. Bilingualism that helps one express one's spiritual experience is cultivated in a similar fashion. Children and their parents need times when they are immersed in the language of their tradition, and they need opportunities to study how religious language works.

Immersion in a Religious Community

The easiest way to be immersed in religious language is to participate as a family in the worship life of a faith community. In the words and actions of a service of worship, participants hear and observe the "grammar" of a tradition. Certain kinds of words and actions are organized and conveyed according to particular conventions and rules inherent to the community and crucial to consistent understanding among those gathered. Experiencing a part of the service, such as the Lord's Prayer (or Our Father) in a Christian service or a traditional blessing at the conclusion of a Jewish Shabbat service week after week renders those words (and their placement in the service) familiar.

Singing the same songs or hymns over time soon means that one can sing at least bits of them from memory. Standing, kneeling, swaying, and opening and closing one's eyes, then repeating this language of movement, teaches our bodies to "speak" the common discourse with particular actions. We may not yet understand what all the words mean or why we move in specific ways, but we have begun to communicate in a given religious language as imitators of that language.

Is this not the primary way very young children learn to communicate? An infant listens as her parents talk and soon begins to repeat the words she hears frequently. A preschooler watches his sibling argue with a friend about whose turn it is to go first on the swing and imitates the older child's tone and vocabulary with his own friends later. A toddler stretches her arms out before the evening meal, communicating to the rest of the family that she wants to join hands and say a blessing, as she has noticed that they do every night. Children are terrific imitators of those around them, but they cannot imitate what is outside their experience. Participating regularly in the worship life of a community of faith provides exposure to religious language that they (and we) can imitate as one aspect of learning to be bilingual.

Sometimes, a bit of parental coaching can help children identify forms of religious language that lend themselves to imitation. During a visit to a Northeastern church, I observed a preschool girl being coached in whispers by her mother, approaching others during the congregation's Passing of the Peace ritual; her hand was outstretched and she was saying, "Peace be with you." Her mother's gentle reminder of what to do and say underscored the importance of this form of ritual communication in their tradition. That most of the people around her also were shaking hands and repeating the same words further reinforced the significance of this communication as a meaningful exchange in her community of faith.

Participating in a worshipping community also contributes to the acquisition of a religious language by conveying the meaning of particular words through the timing, tone, and actions associated with those words in the service. Even if the precise meaning of the word still eludes us, we pick up a sense of its connotations. For the preschool

Helping Children Name God's Presence in Their Lives

girl mentioned earlier, "peace" gets associated with human relationships, carefully chosen words, and reciprocity. She might not be able to define "peace" in relation to "war," but she is experiencing a set of interactions designed to communicate peace making. If this same child should hear a worship leader repeatedly pronouncing a word such as *sin* with a negative inflection, pounding his fist while speaking, she would conclude that sin is something bad or dangerous, even if she was not sure what constitutes a sin. When my daughter, at four, would repeat certain Christian words—*Jesus, hosanna,* and *alleluia,* for example—as she sang during worship, she knew that these words and the act of singing at church were about relating to God because of what she had heard people say and where we were located. She

The Rhythm of Religious Language

Because we don't necessarily think about the sentence structure and linguistic rhythms of either scripture texts or classic children's books when we read them, the similarities in their patterns may not be obvious to us at first. Yet pause and recall Dr. Seuss's *Green Eggs and Ham.* Throughout the book, a couplet appears frequently: "I do not eat green eggs and ham. I do not like them, Sam-I-am." Compare this recurring theme with the pattern set in Psalm 136:

O give thanks to the Lord, for God is good,
    for God's steadfast love endures forever;
O give thanks to the God of gods,
    for God's steadfast love endures forever;
O give thanks to the Lord of lords,
    for God's steadfast love endures forever;
who alone does great wonders,
    for God's steadfast love endures forever;
who by understanding made the heavens,

didn't always remember exactly what the words meant, but she had noticed that they were used a lot in sermons and songs, so they must be important—not a bad bit of detective work on her part, as her choice words are indeed central to the Christian story.

Immersion Through Stories

Telling religious stories also provides children with a linguistic immersion experience. Reading aloud creation stories, psalms, or the New Testament beatitudes, all of which are particularly rhythmic and linguistically repetitive, is the religious equivalent to reading nursery rhymes, Dr. Seuss, and *Goodnight, Moon.* Other good religious texts

> for God's steadfast love endures forever;
> who spread out the earth on the waters,
>   for God's steadfast love endures forever. . . .
>
> The repetition of the second phrase continues as a response to the changing first half of the couplet for another twenty verses, and by the end, the words, "for God's steadfast love endures forever" are caught in the mind as firmly as the declaration by Dr. Seuss's green-eggs-and-ham-hater is by the end of that story.
>
> A similar, more elongated, rhythm occurs in the Genesis 1 telling of the creation story. Each act of creation begins with the words, "And God said. . . ." The description of each day concludes with the appropriate "And there was evening and there was morning, the first [second, third. . .] day." Several times the phrase "and God saw that it was good" follows the naming of particular acts of God's creativity, such as "God made the wild animals of the earth of every kind, and the cattle of every kind, and everything that creeps upon the ground of every kind. And God saw that it was good" (Genesis 1:25).

Helping Children Name God's Presence in Their Lives

are any that claim the attention and imagination of the adult doing the reading, for the adult's engagement with the text communicates itself to the children listening and invites them to adopt the language of the story as their own.

The child's adoption of particular words or phrases from the canon of religious stories may correspond more or less directly with the actual language of the text. Just as children who are learning to recite the English alphabet will slur the middle letters into the phrase "elem minnow p" (instead of "l, m, n, o, p"), children learning a religious language make translation errors, particularly when a religious term sounds like another, more familiar, word in their first language. "Our Father in heaven, Harold be thy name . . ." is a rather common misappropriation of the first two lines of the Lord's Prayer. A young child substitutes the name "Harold" for the unfamiliar "hallowed" because supplying a recognizable name seems to fit the intent of the phrase. Some substitutions, however, are an indication that a child has grasped the meaning of an ancient religious phrase for the contemporary context. I overheard a four-year-old girl spontaneously finish her church school teacher's quotation of a memory verse from Psalm 122. The teacher began the sentence, "I was glad when they said to me. . . ." and her student excitedly called out, "L . . . et's go to church!" The verse as the teacher had conveyed it the week before concludes, ". . . let us go to the house of the Lord!" The child had made the connection, most likely because she had previously heard adults refer to the church as "God's house," between going to the house of the Lord and going to church. Thus her acquisition of religious language also included some shifting of the traditional language into a contemporary dialect.

Rabbi Howard Bogot has pointed out that "children are not only born with the basic liturgical ingredients—wonder, joy, love, drama, and natural spontaneity—but they appreciate the opportunity to transform aspects of their world into personal as well as established declarations concerning God." They learn to label objects and their desires with words learned from their social environment. Their ability to use religious terminology and verbalize an awareness of God depends on their "overhearing" religious language in their primary social settings and "seeing" others apply this religious vocabulary in ways they can imitate.

The ability of even young toddlers to learn religious language and practices through sensory immersion in a religious culture prior to verbal language acquisition was quite apparent in one of my parish ministry settings. This particular congregation had a live audiovisual feed of its worship service in its church nursery. Each Sunday, the infants and young toddlers in the nursery "overheard" the music and spoken words of the liturgy and "saw" their community engage in acts of worship. Those children who attended church frequently showed signs of having learned pieces of the sung liturgy; young toddlers would sing snippets of congregational hymns with the same gusto as simple children's songs. They especially picked up the tunes and words to hymn refrains that contained multiple repetitions of simple phrases. They also would chime in on the last word of each line in a familiar hymn, and what they could not sing verbally they would hum. Parents reported that their almost-two-year-olds were as likely to sing a string of "alleluias" as "Twinkle, Twinkle, Little Star" when moved to song during a shopping expedition or a long car ride. The practical intelligence of these children, combined with their social exposure to religious culture, was sufficient for them to learn and use, albeit without rational comprehension, the religious language of their faith community.

Studying Religious Language

It is important, however, that children learn the meaning of religious words and phrases as well as their pronunciation and timing in a set liturgy, or else their ability to communicate in more sophisticated religious conversations is limited. Here, too, are parallels with general language acquisition. All three of my children have regular spelling and vocabulary tests as part of their schoolwork. Each week, they must pull out a dictionary and find the meaning of between ten and twenty-five new words so they can pass a test on Friday. They write sentences containing these words so they will understand how to use them in context. Despite their complaint that teachers only do this to torment them, the process of learning new words builds the

Spiritual Songs and Hymns for Young Children

Although there are numerous simple religious songs written specifically for children, many songs and hymns of the wider faith community also shape the lives of little ones through their memorable phrases. Consider the classic Christian hymn "Great Is Thy Faithfulness." The refrain repeats the title phrase three times and is itself repeated after each verse of the hymn. Thus a child listening to "Great Is Thy Faithfulness" hears those words ten times in the few minutes it takes to sing the three verses. (The hymn begins with its title phrase as well.) It doesn't take many encounters with such a hymn to imprint a phrase repeated that frequently on a young mind.

Some religious songs employ an echo strategy that invites young children (and all others) to repeat the text. "This Is the Day" is a popular congregational song based on Psalm 118. Each phrase of the song is sung and then echoed by the singers, with the second half of each verse being a nonechoing repetition of the first half. The first verse goes like this:

vocabulary they need to read broadly and describe more precisely what they experience and think. It augments their ability to understand what others are trying to communicate.

The study of religious language can draw on similar tools. Dorling Kindersley has published two detailed story Bibles that function as reference books as well. In the margins of *The Children's Illustrated Bible* and *The Illustrated Jewish Bible for Children* (both by Selena Hastings) are illustrations and explanations of the unfamiliar items and terms used in biblical narratives. Sidebars describe the context of the story, the common lifestyle of the era, and other pertinent information that might illuminate the story's potential meanings. Arche-

This is the day, this is the day
that the Lord has made, that the Lord has made;
we will rejoice, we will rejoice,
and be glad in it, and be glad in it.
This is the day that the Lord has made,
we will rejoice and be glad in it.
This is the day, this is the day
that the Lord has made.

A young child hearing these repetitions quickly begins to pick up the words along with the tune.

Other hymns and songs repeat key words of the faith tradition. "Holy, Holy, Holy! Lord God Almighty" introduces its young hearers to the importance of the word *holy* in the religious lexicon. "Come, Christians, Join to Sing" emphasizes *alleluia* and *amen* by using both words at the end of three out of four lines per stanza. The Jewish Passover song, *Dayenu!* repeats the title term (Hebrew for "it would have been enough") six times in the refrain. In fact, *dayenu* is the only word sung in the refrain, which follows a series of six or more verses recounting God's miraculous intervention on behalf of the Israelites and Jews throughout the ages.

ological photographs of artifacts provide additional glimpses of what a *talent* (a unit of money), an *ephod* (a box containing sacred objects), or a pomegranate tree look like and where they could be found. Other photographs show the contemporary locations of significant places such as Mount Sinai and the Sea of Galilee in Jewish and Christian history. These books resemble the popular *The Way Things Work* and the *Eyewitness* and *Cross-Sections* nonreligious book series in the amount of detail provided to help illuminate the meaning of the people, objects, and events described.

Jewish publishers have developed numerous books designed to explain the special holidays of that tradition—holidays that not only

Helping Children Name God's Presence in Their Lives

continue to be celebrated by Jews today but form the basis for many Christian stories and traditions because of the shared history of the two religions. Jewish Lights, the same company that publishes Sandy Sasso's books, has books for adult readers and materials for adults and children to share. One of my favorites is *Shared Blessings,* which explores the spiritual significance of thirteen Jewish festivals and holy days through contemporary stories and historic information. Kar-Ben has a series of story and prayer books for Yom Kippur (Day of Atonement), Rosh Hashanah (the Jewish New Year), and other Jewish high holy days. These texts provide the liturgy for and explain the traditional rituals of these ancient celebrations in ways that suggest how interfaith families might observe the holidays in a contemporary home.

Christian publishers also distribute reference books that assist adults and children in studying their tradition. Bible guides, atlases, and dictionaries offer background information and define terminology. Many draw on the evolving scholarship of archeologists, historians, sociologists, and theologians, and the best share with their readers the ambiguities that still exist in the scholarly understandings about various events, people, eras, and language translations. Some suggest activities for families to help children draw connections between other time periods and their own culture and family life. Some, like Fiona Walton's *Let's Explore inside the Bible,* provide interesting trivia, such as the varieties of fish in the Sea of Galilee where Jesus' disciples liked to go fishing or the length of wedding celebrations, to capture children's imaginations. Others, such as *The Access Bible* or *The Learning Bible,* provide translations of the Christian scriptures with study notes, charts, maps, and glossaries included alongside the text, either on-line or on CD-ROM. Jewish families can find guidance in the Torah commentaries published by Jewish Lights and others.

School children also gather in reading groups and writing workshops to talk about the literature of their culture and work out its meanings together. They work sentence-by-sentence (if they are young) or chapter-by-chapter (when they are older) to identify unknown words, clarify characters and plot movement, discuss ambiguous meanings, and compare interpretations. They answer set questions about texts and compose paragraphs and essays that demonstrate their comprehension of and creative response to narratives. Sometimes they create artistic expressions of what they've read or written, or they may dramatize a story. Talking with other children about stories and listening to the words their peers choose and the sentences they construct challenges children to make sense of language as it is communicated by others. It also models diverse ways of using language creatively to organize and share one's thoughts.

Church and Hebrew schools, youth groups, after-school kids' clubs, and religious schools can provide this type of structured study environment for exploring religious literature and its language. A typical religious class setting provides children with the opportunity to read and engage with others in an interactive discussion about a story or theme significant to that faith tradition. Good programs use the same philosophy of integrative learning currently popular in public school classrooms, where children do far more than answer fill-in-the-blank questions about a story's content. Comprehensive religious language study involves learning about the origins of unfamiliar words, the historical contexts of stories, the concerns of the authors who wrote the texts, and the implications of all these aspects for how we interpret the meaning of words and stories in our contemporary context. It requires attending to our subjective experience of stories and discussions about stories, as well as our more critical examination of them. When children dramatize the story of Ruth gleaning wheat in the fields of her cousin Boaz, they discover how hard the life of a woman whose survival depended on bending and picking up stray stalks of wheat in order to gather enough to grind flour for a loaf of bread would have been. Their new comprehension of the term *gleaning* gives them greater appreciation for Ruth's perseverance and helps explain her decision to seek marriage with Boaz as a longer-term solution to her own survival and that of her extended family.

Studying together in formal groups also helps children notice and experience the communal aspects of religious language. Many prayers use the plural, "we," in their traditional forms. On Yom Kippur, Jews say, "We have sinned," rather than confess individual shortcomings apart from their collective sense of wrongdoing. Their

79

language emphasizes the weaknesses of all and the shared need for repentance and reconciliation with God and one another. Christians pray, "Give us this day our daily bread," petitioning God for sustenance for all who hunger according to their need. Saying these prayers collectively reinforces in an experiential way the linguistic message of a shared reality inherent in the choice of pronoun. When

Communal Prayers

Mary Batchelor has collected numerous personal and communal prayers in her book *Children's Prayers From Around the World*. Some are written by religious leaders from earlier centuries, such as St. Clement's first-century prayer, "Oh God, make us children of quietness and heirs of peace" and John Wesley's eighteenth-century mealtime grace:

Be present at our table, Lord;
Be here and everywhere adored.
Thy creatures bless and grant that we
May feast in paradise with thee.

Under the theme of thanksgiving, she includes a traditional Jewish table prayer: "Blessed art thou, O Lord our God, Ruler of the universe, who brings forth bread form the earth." Gathered into the set of prayers titled, "God Cares," is this one from Haiti: "Lord, how glad we are that we don't hold you but that you hold us." There are even several prayers written by children, such as this one:

Thank God for rain and the beautiful rainbow colors
And thank God for letting children splash in puddles.

In all, Batchelor includes over two hundred prayers arranged according to forty different themes.

a teacher also draws children's attention to the words *we, us,* and *our* and leads them in wondering about the significance of these choices, he or she fosters greater understanding of the tradition's beliefs and practices through scrutiny of religious language.

Children also learn about their own language when they have opportunities to compare and contrast it with others. My sixth-grade daughter is studying Spanish in middle school, and she frequently remarks on the structural similarity between words in Spanish and English words that mean the same thing. Yet she is constantly vexed by the different sounds the vowels make ("e" sounds like long "a" and "i" like long "e" in Spanish) because most of the letters used in the two languages are identical. Working out the significance of these similarities and differences is giving her a greater understanding of both languages because she cannot simply rely on her intuitive grasp of how a letter sounds or what language a word represents. Instead, she must attend to a host of clues—context, historical roots, accent, spelling, and word form—to recognize which language she is using and communicate as well as possible.

Studying the similarities and differences among various religious traditions provides a parallel opportunity to identify the more subtle details of one's own religious language. Interfaith households negotiate this process more naturally because of the representation of more than one religious tradition within their extended family. However, any family can use books or friendship connections to explore the language and culture of a faith community apart from their own. *Celebrations!*—a beautiful book produced by Dorling Kindersley for UNICEF—highlights the language and practices of several religious festivals around the world. Included are Eid ul-Fitr, the Islamic feast that signals the completion of the month-long fast of Ramadan, Esala Perahera, a Buddhist celebration involving a procession with the Buddha's Tooth Relic, and Diwali, a Hindu festival of light for the god Rama. Variations of the Christian tradition, including Fassika (the name for Easter in the Ethiopian Orthodox Church) and El Dia de los Muertos (a Mexican day of remembrance for the dead), are represented, as are the Jewish festivals of Purim and Hanukkah.

Helping Children Name God's Presence in Their Lives

Jewish families (or interfaith families raising their children in both the Christian and Jewish traditions) will find that studying their religious language involves studying Hebrew, for the religious discourse of Judaism is tied to the language of its origins. Most books about Jewish holy days include the Hebrew rendering of traditional prayers, a phonetic transliteration of the Hebrew text in English, and an English translation. Like preschools that have every item in the classroom labeled with both their English and Spanish (or French) names, this side-by-side provision of both languages helps children make the association between the unfamiliar phrases and the English words they may already recognize. Sunday morning and late-afternoon Hebrew schools provide general instruction in ancient and (sometimes) modern Hebrew, as well as encounters with religious narratives and practices. Children learn to say traditional festival prayers and to recognize the Hebrew names for important religious concepts such as *shalom* (peace, greetings), *tefillah* (prayer), and *tzedakah* (sharing). While learning their religious language, they also acquire some familiarity with a second social language. A similar process occurs for Muslim and Hindu children who participate in parochial schools designed to encourage literacy in the original language of the tradition.

Christian families and congregations can learn from our friends in other religious traditions to create our own parallel naming structures. Although we don't have a second cultural language readily available to us for this work, we do have a host of religious terms and symbolic items that we help our children recognize, compare, and contrast. We can point out that the chalice and paten used during communion are the religious equivalents of our glasses and plates at dinnertime. Don't forget to point out that the tables are similar as well! Using a Bible or religious dictionary, we can talk about how "paraments" (the colored cloths hanging on pulpits, lecterns, and altars) are similar to tablecloths and banners. We can place religious symbols in appropriate places in our homes: a chalice and paten in our dining room to remind us of Jesus' words during the last supper and of the celebration of communion; the word *shalom* by the door to remind us to come and go in peace; a dove in each child's bedroom to signify the presence of the Holy Spirit with us in our waking and our sleeping. In this more limited way, we gain some of the religious benefits that families in other traditions find in the study of an original religious language.

Religious Language and Spiritual Formation

Not every encounter with religious language, however, proves equally beneficial to spiritual formation. Craig Dykstra, in his essay, "Youth and the Language of Faith," says religious language that contributes to the nurture and support of faith formation must be "clear enough to be comprehended by young people, rich enough to be meaningful, concrete enough to relate to the world as it is, and critical enough to keep open the dynamics of inquiry and continuing conversation." Vocabulary or sentence structures that are almost always too complex for a child's cognitive stage, flat intonations and word choices that fail to spark the imagination, lofty phrases implying that spirituality only pertains to ethereal matters, and religious truth claims imposed in an authoritarian fashion stymie spiritual formation. Religious language should invite and equip children and adults to participate in an interesting conversation about issues and concerns that matter in their lives. It isn't something children acquire just so they (or we) can check religion off as another subject mastered on the way to adulthood. It is a communication tool for a meaningful life.

Let's consider each of Dykstra's criteria in turn so we can understand better how religious language best functions in service of that goal.

Clarity

Daily conversation in my household runs the gamut from simple exchanges ("Dad, have you washed my jeans?" "Yes, they're in the dryer.") and directives ("Please get ready for bed.") to more complex discussions about the state of world affairs or the fairness of family

Helping Children Name God's Presence in Their Lives

Four Guiding Principles of Religious Language

Clarity uses terminology and logical reasoning appropriate to the age and developmental stage of the hearers. Everything that a child hears need not be cognitively clear, but a child must have some points of cognitive connection for religious language to be intelligible.

Richness incorporates metaphors and other symbolic language, variations in tone, and combinations of simple and complex grammatical structures. The degree of richness required to hold a child's attention depends on his or her linguistic abilities and personality.

Concreteness evokes a sense of personal relevance through intentional reference to children's experiences, as well as to the experiences of others. Language describing unfamiliar experiences can be rendered relevant by drawing attention to the implicit connections between the unknown and the known.

Critical Awareness makes room for analysis and inquiry, while providing a framework within which to ask, "Why?" Not having all the answers encourages children to explore possibilities and make up their own minds.

rules. No matter where we are on that conversation continuum, however, the ages of the children involved affect the way my husband and I structure our language to communicate what we mean. For example, for our eight-year-old, we provide shorter instructions and repeat them often to help him stay on task. And our eleven-year-old gets frustrated if we offer homework tips that differ from her teachers' explanations, because she finds an alternative approach confusing rather than illuminating. For her, we try to match the vocabulary and logical structure of the language she's heard at school. Our fifteen-year-old enjoys the art of debate and will argue a point for the sheer pleasure of the verbal battle, so we pay more attention to the precise meaning of our words when we interact with him. And on evenings when a friend's toddler comes to stay with us, we communicate as much by body language as with short sentences and simple words.

The clarity of our communication depends on our respecting the linguistic and psychosocial capabilities of all participants. We have to match our vocabulary, our sentence structure, and our communication style to the needs of our children so that they hear what we mean rather than simply a collection of sounds or words without meaning. We have to talk on their level.

Thus clarity in our religious speech requires that we consider the linguistic capabilities of the children with whom we are talking. With young children, we teach basic vocabulary by naming religious items and experiences repeatedly, identifying our day of worship as "Sabbath," prayer before meals as "table grace," and acts of compassion as "following Jesus" or enacting "shalom." We can also use repetition and visual cues to help them craft prayers for personal or communal use. In one of my congregations, a group of preschool children composed prayers of thanksgiving by cutting out magazine pictures of things they have or use each day. Before they began, their teachers had talked with them about the things we need to be healthy and serve God well. They then glued pictures onto a large piece of poster board on which were printed the words, "Thank you, God, for _____" several times. The children shared their prayer in congregational worship, and the teachers cut up the poster afterward so each child could take home one line as a reminder to give thanks to God. The simplicity of this exercise matched the vocabulary and linguistic capabilities of these young children, resulting in clear communication between the teachers and the children about prayer.

As children's skills in their cultural language grow, we begin to encourage them to retell stories from their faith tradition in their own words. Sometimes this might include literally asking them to tell back to us a biblical story that we have just read from the Bible or a Bible storybook together. But more often, encouraging them involves inviting them to talk with us about the ways in which they see Bible

Helping Children Name God's Presence in Their Lives

stories coming alive around them. We might ask them to begin categorizing their daily experiences in terms of theological themes: When did they receive or offer hospitality? What gives them hope? Where is there a need for repentance? Then as their ability to analyze an argument develops, we might offer nuanced explanations for our own spiritual commitments and invite the same from our children. My family spent a lot of time talking about the events of September 11, 2001 and about our family's stance with regard to the war in Iraq. We puzzled together over the meaning of our faith tradition's stories and their implications for our responses to these crisis events as well as our daily living. Often these conversations took place at the dinner table, but nearly as often one of our children would comment on something they had heard at school or on the radio. Long before I saw a bumper sticker that read, "God bless the world," my children had raised questions about the "fairness" of the phrase "God bless America" and wondered aloud whether God wouldn't prefer us to seek blessing for everyone. Hence, clarity can also be about letting our children set the agenda for the focus of our conversation and then sticking with the topic they propose.

At the same time, when we communicate with the family as a whole, we speak on several levels at once in order to convey our meaning to everyone. We craft our speech in such a way that everyone's capabilities are addressed in some part of the communication. We do not simply address household members collectively as if all function at the same level as the youngest among us. Such "talking down" would likely generate misunderstanding, especially from the teenager whose meaning-making process is sensitized to developmental slights. Instead, we communicate our message in multiple phrases, some of which are intended primarily for the eight-year-old's ears and others of which are designed to elicit a response from the teen, or the middle school child, or the adult spouse. The use of a multiplicity of forms to convey the same content respects the different personalities and developmental capabilities of each family member. It also presumes that talk that is over some family members' heads or beneath the capabilities of other members is acceptable as long as other parts of the communication are tailored to their needs.

REAL KIDS, REAL FAITH

Admittedly, it can be difficult to figure out how consciously to do this in religious conversation, because we often engage in multi-level conversations as part of our routine of getting through the day and so don't really think about how it is happening. The trick is to think about the common aspects of your various children's interests and activities that might relate to the question or issue at hand, just as you would if you were trying to convince them to listen to your admonition to get ready for school or behave appropriately during a family reunion. For instance, in talking about the "God bless America" rhetoric and my children's questions about whether it was appropriate, I used simple sports analogies about "nice" and "mean" ways of rooting for your favorite team with my youngest son, who loves soccer. I asked my middle school daughter how such rhetoric made her feel and why, since I knew she was learning in school about "finding your voice," and I asked my teenager what he thought was at stake in choosing to use or not use such rhetoric along with his friends, knowing that peer relationships are very important at his age. We also talked about the pros and cons of using the phrase; the children articulated their ideas according to the logic of their own concerns and capabilities, but all could understand the idea of "pluses" and "minuses." Some of the teenager's ideas were far more philosophical than the youngest could understand, but including everyone's ideas meant that all three children were part of the conversation and felt heard.

This same approach to clarity amidst diversity is necessary if communal religious experiences such as worship are to speak clearly to children of various ages as well as adults. Some of the words used should be cognitively accessible to young children, but the whole service need not exclusively use the vocabulary of a five-year-old. Specialized theological terms can be used and then defined in more than one way so that a broader cross-section of worshippers can make sense of them. Body language can be employed to reinforce the intended meaning of a statement nonverbally. The intentional repetition of words and phrases that children have heard elsewhere, or even in previous services of worship, can draw them in along with adults. Sophisticated arguments can appeal to teenage and adult skeptics, while

Helping Children Name God's Presence in Their Lives

coexisting alongside statements that summarize a point in a simple illustration that speaks to younger children or commonsense-oriented adults. Clarity in religious language is about intentionally varying our speech patterns so that everyone can hear what the tradition might have to say.

Richness

I have an adult friend who likes to relax by coloring. She has a case full of crayons in graduated shades of every color imaginable and coloring books of intricate black-and-white images waiting for her artistic touches. She carefully plans her color schemes and applies them to the pages with an eye toward creating a finished work that has depth and beauty. Her coloring lends richness to an otherwise flat image, rendering it more interesting to her and to those who behold it when it is done.

The richness of religious language comes in part from the color we give it through the use of metaphorical images, carefully chosen synonyms, variations in speaking tone, and intentional shading of our meaning through the structure of phrases and organization of sentences. The degree of richness necessary to appeal to our children depends in part on their ages. Just as a toddler who is only beginning to learn about color is quite happy with a set of four (red, yellow, blue, green) crayons, very young children require more simplicity and consistency of language than variation. Retelling traditional stories in simple sentences, naming the parts of communal celebrations and identifying religious items, and repeating common prayers and greetings satisfy their meaning-making needs. Preschoolers who are ready to take on the adventure of an eight- or sixteen-crayon box need to hear more details about the traditional stories they've heard so their picture of it becomes more colorful. They are able to begin noticing the interpretive claims that outline the story images and set boundaries around how enthusiastically one can apply one's one own interpretive "color" before going outside the lines. Being imaginative thinkers, they need religious language to provide some latitude for experimentation. Their response to a religious event or experience may indicate that they see different possibilities for making meaning than the adults around them. It's like coloring the cow in the farm scene with green polka dots just to see what difference it makes to the picture. Their magical thinking contends with their desire to please others through conformity, and they require a sufficiently large set of religious words and stories to fuel their imaginative play.

As children's awareness of the world's complexity grows, the size of their religious box of linguistic crayons needs to keep pace. More advanced cognitive abilities require both the subtle and sensual appeal of metaphorical language and the logical beauty of well-reasoned arguments to pique their interest. When my eight-year-old leans over during a sermon and whispers in my ear, "Mom, he just keeps saying the same thing over and over again; doesn't he think we get it?" he is complaining that the religious language he's hearing isn't rich enough to encourage additional meaning making. He needs a new lens through which to view religious ideas, one that breaks open his thinking in a new and challenging way. Teens are particularly vulnerable to being turned off by religious language that has become so definitional and rote in use that it has lost its experimental possibilities. If they begin to complain that religion is boring, perhaps it's time to introduce them to some of the saints and martyrs of the faith whose graphic stories expand on the central biblical stories we usually tell. Maybe we need to invite them to help us find new analogies and metaphors for the values we're trying to communicate and the characteristics we hope to cultivate. I wish I'd thought to whisper back to my son, "If you were preaching, what else would you say about this story?" We both might have gained a richer appreciation for the gospel that day if I had.

Concreteness

Children begin using language as a tool for naming the people and things around them. As they grow, they describe their world in greater detail and begin to grasp abstract concepts as well as the more tangible aspects of daily living. Yet children and youth remain strongly attached to the need to see the personal relevancy of information and experiences if they are to engage them seriously. Frankly, most adults feel the same way! We want to know what something has to do with *us,* why it matters in *our* lives, what its implications are for *our* future. Taken to the extreme of disregard for the significance of an event for those around us as well as ourselves, this concern becomes self-centeredness. But understood as an aspect of the human condition in which we long to understand the relationship between ourselves and the rest of the world, this desire signals an appropriate concern for concreteness. Religious language that is concrete supplies explanations, metaphors, ritual phrases, and narratives that help persons of any age recognize the connections between the divine and the ordinary.

Rabbi Bogot suggests that one way to speak concretely about God's presence in the world with young children is to create a "God's Creation Viewing Station" at one window in the family home. At regular intervals (daily, weekly), the child looks out that window and draws a picture of a natural object he or she sees. The parent, using the language of "God's creation," reinforces the connection between the objects in this world and God's creativity. New bulbs springing up in the garden are no longer simply flowers; they are the daffodils that God made. A sunset becomes an experience of the beauty of God's light as well.

Even without a designated window, adults can call attention to ways in which God is made known in the world. Rabbi Bogot calls this "identifying those experiences that 'advertise' sacred time" or sacred actions. In my household, we talk about how the volunteers who respond to disasters with humanitarian aid are working as "God's hands and feet." We know that the people doing the work may not share our faith tradition; indeed, they may not consider themselves religious at all. But the work they are doing fits our understanding of the kind of compassion God desires for persons in need. They are a sign of God's care for the world through the people God created, even as they remain volunteers of whatever organization they represent. One interpretation does not negate the other; they are simply two different ways of speaking about two different cultural realities.

Children who are becoming religiously bilingual will initiate concrete conversation about God's relationship to the world, particularly if the adults around them encourage such talk. I mentioned in Chapter Two that my eldest child, when three, believed that God participated in our games of catch by intercepting the ball at the top of its upward arc and throwing it back down to earth. He spontaneously shared this perception while we were playing one day. I can only imagine what wheels had been turning in his head as he observed the trajectory of the ball and wondered why it moved first upward and then downward without an obvious human intervention in its direction. I remember thinking at the time that perhaps I should tell him gravity, not God, was responsible for the ball's arc. The words I settled on, however, were that "God uses gravity to make the ball act that way." My explanation linked the religious and the scientific in a way that permitted my son to believe in both as active forces in his environment.

Critical Awareness

The tension between religious and scientific (or religious and humanitarian) explanations for events in our world is one reason we must use religious language that leaves room for critical inquiry. The unrelenting "Why?" of a toddler gives us an early indication that children are naturally inquisitive about their world. Children wonder why God made the sky blue and the grass green, why we light candles on special occasions, why we go to church or synagogue when the child next door stays home, and why we take canned goods to the local food pantry.

Older elementary children who have moved into the "scientific inquiry" stage press harder at the inconsistencies between what they hear people say about their religious beliefs and how those same people live out their spiritual commitments. They ask tough questions about how God works in the world. My daughter, at age nine, turned to me in the car after a church service and asked, "Why did God let Bekah get cancer?" The minister had used a sermon illustration about a child with cancer that moved my daughter to think about her own friend who was undergoing chemotherapy. She wanted to understand how God, whom she believed to be all-powerful and a healer, could permit a child to have a life-threatening illness. Our ensuing conversation about the brokenness of the world and God's grief over the sickness and tragedy that come from the breakdown of our environment and the accidents of biology was an important point in her evolving interpretation of the kind of power and presence God has in the world. She was moving away from her sense of God as a magical being to a new understanding of God as someone or something in relationship with the world in a more complicated way. She could imagine becoming a partner with this "new" God, who desired to have the "hands and feet" of ordinary people in this world working to share God's love in times of health and illness. She (and I) will spend a lifetime working out the tension between our belief in God's power and our experience of brokenness (what some would call evil) in the world. When we teach our children a religious language that encourages such questioning, we create a space for ongoing interpretation and meaning making in our children's lives as well as our own.

Chapter 5

PRAYING WITH CHILDREN

❧❖❧

Most us, when we think of prayer, think first of talking to God rather than sitting in silence. We may be aware of various famous prayers: the Lord's Prayer (the Our Father), the Passover Kiddush (blessing), the Prayer of St. Francis ("Lord, make me an instrument of your peace"), or the Muslim *Allahu Akbar* ("God is Great"). We may have engaged in intercessory prayer, in which we sought God's help in some situation or for someone. Perhaps our families shared a table grace or a bedtime prayer when we were children. When I was growing up, the primary set prayer of my childhood was a mealtime prayer:

> Come, Lord Jesus, be our guest,
> and let this food to us be blessed. Amen.

Occasionally, this prayer would be supplanted by more folksy prayers like the Johnny Appleseed prayer I learned to sing in church camp:

> The Lord is good to me, and so I thank the Lord
> for giving me the things I need,
> the sun and the rain and the apple seed.
> The Lord is good to me.

Many adults can still recite the words to table graces or nighttime prayers such as "Now I lay me down to sleep" because these prayers were said every day in their household. The association of words with prayer is an appropriate connection to make, yet that association also obscures the powerful spiritual aspects of silence.

Roberta Bondi, a religious historian and spiritual guide, talks about prayer as "a shared life with God." This shared life includes our speech about the events and concerns of our days, but it does not end there. In order to make room for God's presence, we must create spaces empty of our own noise and invite God to "speak" to us in the silence. This is what my children's Quaker school set out to do in their silent meeting for worship each week, and we can provide similar opportunities for silence for children at home and in religious communities. But first we have to face our own ambivalences about silence, both in terms of the role silence plays in our own lives and in light of our assumptions about children's ability to be silent.

THE ROLE OF SILENCE

Silence is uncommon in the busy lives of contemporary parents. Young children chatter at us about their activities; National Public Radio or the songs and patter of a music station accompany us on our daily errand and chauffeur runs, and the blare of commercials punctuates the talk shows and dramas with which we entertain ourselves on television. We may exercise with headphones piping more talk and music into our lives. We stay tuned in while we cook and clean, or we combine chores with conversations about homework, tomorrow's schedule, and all the other details that demand our attention. A computerized bell dinging alerts us to the arrival of another e-mail message or an appointed conversation. Beeping watch alarms remind us to pick up the kids from soccer or dance class. All these distractions from silence may be welcome buffers against the interior noise we realize we will have to contend with if things get too quiet.

For many of us, our interior lives can be just as noisy. We operate with mental to-do lists that we run through and tick off repeatedly during the day. We may negotiate feelings of anxiety, guilt, frustration, and annoyance through internal dialogues designed to sort out our emotional response and come to some resolution of the conflict we're experiencing. Plans to ask for time off from work or a different arrangement of household tasks frequently get rehearsed in our heads before we say them out loud. Even in our sleep, we may toss and turn when the burden of balancing household, work, and self-interests seems unmanageable. Silence hardly seems to be our friend.

Yet it is precisely in these times that God can befriend us in silence that is practiced as a discipline rather than a happenstance. The disciplined use of silence as a means of listening for divine wisdom helps us clear the clutter and noisiness from our lives long enough to allow another sense of what could be to take shape in our thoughts and imagination. This other sense may be nothing more than a heightened awareness that God dwells with us in the midst of ordinary tasks and extraordinary dilemmas, or it may be greater clarity about a particular action we need to take in our lives. We may feel as if we are resting peacefully in a warm embrace or being propelled, with God's help, into more intense and courageous engagement with the very person or thing we fear. The gifts of silence are varied; what they have in common is their availability to any who will diligently seek them out.

However, because our own experiences of silence can be ambivalent, we may hesitate to encourage our children to seek out silence for themselves. We also tend to characterize children as too active and undisciplined to remain still and silent for any productive length of time. A group of church school teachers responsible for working with older elementary students told me after I visited their classroom that they struggled with using the periods of silence advocated in their curriculum because it seemed abnormal for third and fourth graders to refrain from socializing with one another. As a culture, we assume that preschool children are natural chatterboxes, which leads us to treat silence in the next room with suspicions about what kind of trouble the children are getting into.

Most adults can justify asking children to be quiet while adults are talking because being quiet is a basic principle of polite social behavior and recognizes the culturally defined social authority of adults over children. But we also wonder if expecting children to sit silently in contemplation is insensitive or inhumane, given their lack of personal and social maturity. We forget that even very young children will sit mesmerized by the movement of a ceiling fan or turn a rattle over and over as they examine its shape, color, texture, taste, and sound quality. The flicker of a candle flame captivates a child's eye, and the soothing words of a guided meditation are a staple tool of child psychologists who work with children who have been traumatized. We know all too well the temper tantrums and whining of overstimulated children, yet fear that silence will leave them understimulated. We need to question the validity of this fear. Far from being deprived by the intentional creation of silence in their lives, children need times of intentional quietness and stillness to remain in touch with their spirit and the divine force that animates them.

For several years, my three children attended a Quaker school in Massachusetts. Each Tuesday morning, in their individual rooms, they would join their pre-K through eighth-grade classmates in a half-hour silent meeting for worship. Their teachers would light a candle and place it in the center of the circle of seated children. Sometimes a teacher would read a story or place a picture beside the candle. He or she might pose a question for the children to ponder or play a musical piece as a prelude to the silence. Teachers of the youngest children frequently passed out small balls of clay for their students to knead, stretch, and shape quietly as they sat cross-legged on the floor. For about twenty minutes, the only sounds in the school were the soft noises of relaxed breathing and of bodies occasionally shifting position. The spell would eventually be broken by the teachers' invitation to share quietly with one another what had come to them in the silence or to note in their personal journals something of their interior journey during the preceding minutes.

My oldest child participated in this Tuesday ritual of silent prayer for six years before we moved to Indiana. One day, only a few weeks into the year in his new school, he remarked at dinner that he had never expected to be saying this, but what he missed most about his old school was silent meetings for worship. He had found in the regular practice of communal silence a place where he could reflect on the meaning of the events and relationships that made up his days. In the silence, he could ponder his purpose in life and wrestle with the values and commitments he felt called upon to embrace within his various communities. Only in the loss of that ritual did he begin to realize for himself what religious people throughout the ages have known: silence is an essential part of the spiritual life.

Centering Prayer

One form of intentional silence is centering prayer. Its purpose is to help us deal with the noise that distracts us when we seek simply to be in God's presence. It is structured with four movements: preparation, centering, dealing with distraction, and returning. Preparation involves selecting a particular word or phrase that serves to focus our attention on God. The kindergarten and first-grade children in my church school class a few years ago decided that "Jesus loves me, this I know" would be a good phrase for them to use. Familiar with the children's hymn from which these words come, they could repeat it slowly over and over in their minds, lips moving silently, as they moved into the actual process of centering themselves. An adult friend uses "Mother God, come to me" as her usual phrase, breathing rhythmically in on "Mother God" and out on "come to me." (This rhythmic breathing is why some people call this a breath prayer.) Words commonly used are *mercy, shalom* (peace), and *Abba* (Father).

To engage in centering prayer, we close our eyes and repeat our chosen word or phrase silently and slowly for a period of time, using the rhythmic simplicity of the words to focus our attention on an inward movement to meet the center of being. During this time, distractions inevitably arise: an itchy nose, competing thoughts, and external noises such as traffic outside the window or people talking in the next room. We deal with these distractions by gently recalling the mind to its chosen phrase whenever we notice our attention is straying. Learning to focus inwardly on our spiritual center means redirecting ourselves, much the way a parent redirects a toddler whose energy is being exerted in an unhelpful way. That toddler eventually begins to repeat parental instructions to him- or herself—

Praying with Children

"no touch stove, touch toys"—as a form of self-redirection. In centering prayer, we and our children guide ourselves back to God by repeating the "directive" we've provided for ourselves in our chosen word or phrase.

The final movement in centering prayer is returning from our inward center to the world around us. If we try to shift gears abruptly from the stillness of our mind to the noisiness of the world around us, we are likely to feel disoriented by the sudden stimulation. Instead, we slowly let the sounds of the world penetrate our consciousness, opening our eyes when we are ready to take in the external scene and sometimes even shifting our bodies or stretching to awaken relaxed muscles. Whether we have given five minutes or half an hour to this practice of silence, time spent sitting quietly in God's presence provides a sense of being connected to something far greater than ourselves. Moving deep inside ourselves also moves us outside ourselves, centering us and orienting us toward God.

Practicing centering prayer with young children requires persistence and repetition. Begin by talking about simple religious words or phrases that the child knows and likes. Pick a word or phrase together that the child is willing to repeat over and over again for a minute. Practice saying the word or phrase slowly together, and show the child how he can breathe in during the first part of the saying and out during the second part. If necessary, practice breathing slowly together before adding in the words. Once you and your child have practiced a bit, ask him to close his eyes and say the chosen word or phrase aloud with you until you say it is time to stop. Keep time for one minute, breathing and speaking slowly together. Then invite your child to open his eyes and talk with you about how he feels inside after praying in this way. Follow this brief routine several times a week, gradually increasing the time spent in prayer to four or five minutes. If your child is capable of repeating the words to himself, encourage him to do so after several joint sessions. Children who are eight or nine or older can begin by saying the words in their heads, and some are capable of working their way up to thirty minutes or more of silence, particularly if they are a more introverted personality type.

A Guide to Centering Prayer

As you and your children try out the practice
of centering prayer, use the following summary of the four
movements to guide you through the practice.

1. *Preparing.* Choose a sacred word or phrase as the symbol
   of your desire to welcome God's presence and action
   within you.
2. *Centering.* Repeat that word or phrase to focus your attention on God.
3. *Dealing with distraction.* As you become aware of extrane-
   ous thoughts, move yourself back to your chosen word or
   phrase.
4. *Returning.* Slowly bring yourself back to the world
   around you by opening your eyes and beginning to focus
   on the space around you.

Meditative Prayer

Although children younger than ten or twelve can practice the discipline of centering prayer for short periods of time, their concrete
thought patterns incline them more easily toward forms of silence that
intentionally engage the imagination rather than seek to clear the
mind of all images and ideas. Even adults, long schooled by a rational and visual culture to conceptualize ideas as images rather than set
them aside for the intuitive space of emptiness, can find centering
prayer more difficult than meditative prayer. The Quaker school my
children attended strove to provide a variety of imaginative prompts
for silent meditation. These prompts—a poem, a piece of artwork, a
musical selection, a saying—established a loose structure within
which the children could ponder the mysteries of life and their beliefs,
values, and commitments. Thus instead of seeking to clear the mind

of images through the repetition of a single word or phrase so that God can enter the emptiness, meditative prayer provides an image or series of images that guide the one who prays into an encounter with the divine in the imagination.

Praying with Poetry   When we pray by meditating on a poem or excerpt from a book, we are choosing to reflect on our own spiritual experience by pondering the words others have used to interpret their spiritual experiences. My own children love the poetry of Shel Silverstein, author of *Falling Up* and *Where the Sidewalk Ends*. In the introduction to the latter, Silverstein invites those who dream, wish, hope and pray to "Come in!" His poems use a Dr. Seuss-like humor to invite reflection on the difference between the "mustn'ts" and what's really possible ("Listen to the Mustn'ts"), the relationship of humanity to creation ("Invention" and "Forgotten Language"), the sometimes ambiguous nature of help ("Helping"), and the boredom of perpetual happiness ("The Land of Happy"). The concluding poem in the *Sidewalk* volume, "The Search," addresses the human quest for success and raises questions about what it means to have a purpose in life.

Children can read such poems to themselves or listen to them read aloud and then sit quietly, noticing what images and ideas the poetry stirs in them. Parents can encourage this quiet reflection by asking children to close their eyes and try to "picture" the poem in their head while they listen. (When children are reading to themselves, they can pause after each line or verse and close their eyes to "see" what appears.) After a time of silent contemplation, they might draw a picture or write a few sentences in a journal about their response to the poem. If their meditation occurs in tandem with other members of their household or a group, they might choose to share their reflections with one another.

My favorite contemporary poet for the purposes of meditative prayer is Maya Angelou. Her ability to name vulnerability as both challenge and gift moves me, comforts me, and pricks me into more loving action. I have turned to her poem "Tears" for reflection when I craved a word to speak to my periodic experiences of loss and grief.

Tears
The crystal rags
Viscous tatters
of a worn-through soul.
Moans
Deep swan song
Blue farewell
of a dying dream.

Meditating on these words allows me to let Maya Angelou's experience speak for my own experience at a time when I have no words adequate to express my inner turmoil. Her verses bring me to a deeper recognition of what it means to dream and be disappointed ("Tears"), to wonder about the lack of love in the world ("Is Love"), to contemplate the dangers of detachment ("The Detached"), or to explore the challenge of contending with my own and others' hatred and devaluation ("Still I Rise"). Some of my male friends and colleagues find similar solace and challenge in the poetry of R. S. Thomas and Mark Jarman. A musician friend draws on the work of James Weldon Johnson, an African American poet most famous for writing *God's Trombones* and the black national anthem, "Lift Every Voice and Sing."

Praying with Art   Praying with art is similar to meditating on a poem. The artist provides us with a visual interpretation of an idea, experience, or scene and invites us to see in or beyond the object something more intangible than the object itself. The subject of the artwork need not be explicitly religious for us to engage it in an internal spiritual dialogue. I still remember my first encounter with Andy Warhol's 1960s pop art piece, "100 Campbell's Soup Cans." A college professor flashed on screen an image of one hundred identical cans of tomato soup stacked neatly one on top of another and side-by-side for my classmates and me to contemplate as an example of artistic social commentary. The wallpaper-like quality of the image, its familiarity and yet its unnerving repetitiveness, sparked all kinds of questions in my mind. I no longer remember the particular issue with which Warhol's painting helped me wrestle that day, but the sensation of being called into and out of myself by an image continues to be a powerful part of my spiritual journey.

My preadolescent daughter is herself an artist and draws her inspiration from the Impressionists, especially Claude Monet. My eight-year-old son favors "Starry Night" and other works by Vincent van Gogh. My teenager is drawn to the geometric shapes of contemporary and graphic arts. Although these are their favorite types of art for contemplation because of the aesthetic pleasure their forms provide, I invite them to consider a variety of artistic works as part of our family exploration of spirituality. We purchase postcard reproductions of paintings when we visit museums so we can take images home with us for private meditation.

One way to encourage children to pray with art is to purchase an art book of religious images and look at it together. (Although any artwork can be spiritually instructive, novices usually find it easier to start with religious pieces, since their spiritual content is more obvious.) The National Gallery in London has produced a small paperback, *Heaven in Art,* which is an inexpensive option for beginners. It includes close-up sections of paintings, as well as images of the whole, which helps children notice details they might otherwise miss. Before praying, talk about one of the paintings in the book. Read any background information provided; older children might enjoy looking up additional information on the Internet. Once you've piqued your children's interest in the painting, invite them to sit quietly with the book and look carefully at the painting for a few minutes. (With younger children, sit and look together as you would when reading a storybook aloud.) Have them ask the painting, "What message do you have for me?" or "What can you tell me about God?" or "Can you show me a way to be faithful?" Karen Stone, author of *Image and Spirit: Finding Meaning in Visual Art,* suggests questions such as, "Is there a story the artist seems to be telling?" and "What story could I make up about this artwork?" Children can share the responses they receive to these questions with the family or in a journal. Young children may find it easier to draw a picture of the images and ideas that a piece of art creates in them.

Praying with Music   Music is yet another resource for meditative prayer. My younger son loves to listen to Gustav Holst's "The Planets" and visualize the grandeur of the universe. Sometimes he spins and dances around the living room, caught up in the movement of the symphony and his own imagination. Such meditation moves beyond a strict interpretation of contemplation as an engagement in silence, for the introduction of music breaks literal silence. (Indeed, the introduction of poetic words also breaks literal silence, at least temporarily.) Yet music can lead us away from the noise of the external world's chatter and our own internal dissonance to a place where we may encounter God. We can use music as a preparatory device that focuses our attention toward God and paves the way for silent contemplation, or we can make music the form and substance of our meditation. Brother Roger, the French founder and leader of the worldwide Taizé worship movement, encourages the repetitive singing of short, simple songs designed to lead the mind and heart into dialogue with a basic spiritual truth. An introduction to one of the Taizé songbooks that is popular in the United States explains,

> As the words are sung over many times, this reality gradually penetrates the whole being. And these simple songs then enable us to keep on praying when we are alone, by day, by night, and sometimes in the silence of our hearts when we are at work.

Last year during the Christian season of Lent, my daughter and I arose early each Sunday morning and drove downtown to participate in a six-week series of Taizé worship services. Between these gatherings, the songs would remain "stuck in our heads" (as my daughter put it) like a jingle from a radio or television commercial. But unlike the jingle, which one would rather not remember so clearly, we appreciated the echo of "Jesus, remember me" and "In the Lord I'll be ever thankful." The reverberation of these words within us continued to draw us closer to God and to remind us of what God would have us do in our daily living.

Guide to Praying through the Arts

Meditative prayer using poetry, artwork, and music involves focusing one's attention on the words, images, or sounds as guides into the presence of God. In this practice, one lingers in the company of the chosen work, repeating it over in one's mind or holding it in one's gaze the way one appreciatively inspects a gift from a close friend. It can be helpful to remember that each art form is an expression of another's encounter with the spiritual realm.

Praying with Poetry meditating on the words others have used to interpret their spiritual experiences.

Praying with Art meditating on another's visual interpretation of the spiritual life.

Praying with Music meditating on a musical exploration of spiritual themes and experiences in the life of the composer.

John Wesley, one of the founders of Methodism, was a prolific hymn writer. In the introduction to a volume of Christian hymns published in 1791, he provided a set of "Directions for Singing" that United Methodists can still find reprinted in the front of their most recent hymnal. His seventh and last piece of advice is this: "Above all sing spiritually. Have an eye to God in every word you sing." The same might be said of a meditative practice of listening to music: listen spiritually, with an eye toward God in every sound we hear.

Guided Meditation

Sometimes it is easier to learn to meditate if we have verbal cues to guide our imagination into an engagement with a text, image, or musical selection. Psychologists have developed a host of guided meditations to help with stress reduction and personal decision making. These often begin, "Imagine yourself in a beautiful place . . ." (a lush, deep forest or a tropical paradise) or "Imagine yourself living with this person five years from now . . ." The spiritual practice of guided meditation takes a similar approach. We can invite our children (and ourselves) to walk through a story by pausing at intervals in our reading or telling of it to say, "Imagine you are (a particular character in the story). How do you feel? What do you wish you could do next?" Or we might pose a question before playing an instrumental piece of music: "Imagine this music is going to carry you someplace very different from here. What does this new place look like? Where do you see God in this new place?" When the tempo or mood of the music shifts, we might ask, "Now where is the music taking you?" or "What do you imagine God doing now?" Sandy Sasso's interfaith book for children, *God's Paintbrush,* provides similar cues for imagining with our children God's creative activity in the world and our faithful response.

RECLAIMING THE PRACTICE OF LAMENT

As a child, I was taught to bow my head, close my eyes, and fold my hands in my lap when I prayed. This, I was told, was the proper way to show respect for God and thankfulness for all God had done for me, including God's great gift of forgiveness for my sins. From the usual ways I was taught to communicate with God, I learned to view prayer as a duty, an arena for giving thanks and for seeking help with my weaknesses and a time for polite formalities and patient resignation to God's will. It never would have occurred to me to complain to God or to demand things from God; such actions would have seemed disrespectful and bordering on ungratefulness and sinfulness.

Yet many of the prayers we encounter in the common texts of the Jewish, Christian, and Muslim scriptures are precisely these kinds of complaining, demanding prayers. More than one-third of the biblical psalms are laments. One entire book of the Hebrew scriptures—the book of Lamentations—is devoted to lament. Ancient religious peoples recognized that polite prayer requests serve only to limit a person's relationship with God to polite conversation. Praying in the

A Biblical Story for Guided Meditation

Stories from the scriptures can be excellent resources for guided meditation. An adult or older child can read the story aloud from the Bible or a Bible storybook, pausing every few sentences to insert instructions for listeners to imagine themselves as characters in the scene or action just described. Next is a portion of a story about a wise judgment made by the Jewish King Solomon (1 Kings 3:16–28) from Ralph Milton's *The Family Story Bible.* The questions I have provided to accompany this text can easily be modified to fit other stories. They should be asked slowly, with pauses between each question so that the listeners' imaginations have time to work. Afterward you can share your responses to the questions with one another if you want to do so.

A Very Wise King

 . . .Solomon became famous because he was so wise. He always knew what to do with a hard problem.

Imagine you are King Solomon. How does it feel to be famous for your wisdom? Do you enjoy helping people sort out their problems? Do you ever worry about making a mistake?

One day, two women came to him. They lived together in the same house. And they brought a small baby with them. "This is my baby," said the first woman. "It's mine!" said the other. "Wait a bit," said King Solomon. "Tell me what happened." "Both of us had brand new babies," said the first woman. "But the other woman's baby died. Then she took my baby and said it was hers." "I did not," said the second woman. "This is my baby."

Imagine you are one of the women. How do you feel about babies? How do you feel about the other woman? What do you want Solomon to do for you? What do you want Solomon to tell the other woman?

"Well," said King Solomon. "I'll take my sword and I'll cut the baby in two. Then you can each have half a baby." "Sure. Why not?" said the second woman. "No! No!" screamed the first woman. "Give the baby to her. Don't cut it in half. Please!"

Imagine you are King Solomon. Why do you say you are going to cut the baby in half? Now imagine you are the woman who agrees to King Solomon's plan. What are you thinking? How do you feel? Imagine you are the woman who cries, "No!" What are you thinking? How do you feel? Return again to imagining you are King Solomon. What do you think about the two women's reactions? What would you do next?

"Now I know who the baby really belongs to," said King Solomon. He picked up the baby and handed it gently to the first woman. She was the one who said, "Give the baby to her." "I can tell that you are the real mother," said the King, "because you showed that you loved this baby."

Imagine that you are the woman who has been given the baby. What are you feeling? What do you want to say to King Solomon? Imagine you are the other woman. How are you feeling? What do you want to say to King Solomon? Imagine you are King Solomon. What do you want to say to the baby's mother? What do you want to say to the woman who claimed to be the baby's mother?

form of a lament offers children and adults a way to acknowledge the real pain, confusion, and suffering that are a part of our human conditions, while still claiming a place in the realm of God and the reality of God's love and compassion.

A prayer of lament is made up of at least five components; the first involves invoking God's presence, usually through direct address. "Dear God," "Our Father," "Divine Spirit," and "Blessed are you, Lord God" are all forms of invocation. As adults, we might select a form of address that represents our current understanding of who God is or how God acts in the world and help our children do the same from their own perspective. In the second component, we name the disappointments and despairing events in our lives. Here we acknowledge the difficulties we're having with a coworker, the argument with a spouse that has left us seething, the anxiety about neighborhood violence or world hunger. We invite our children to name the sibling rivalries, grade disappointments, fears about bullying, feelings of inadequacy, and concerns for social justice that create stress in their lives. The little boy who is grieving over the death of his pet hamster tells God how bereft he feels. The preadolescent girl who feels left out of the popular clique at school pours out her sorrow in detail. Nothing is withheld from God out of politeness, including one's frustration with God about the situation.

The third element is expressing confidence or trust in the promise of God's responsive love. Here we remember in prayer some of the times and ways that God has cared for God's people—us included—in the past. Maybe we recall a biblical story about God's deliverance of someone in need. Jews and African American Christians often turn to the story of the Israelites' exodus from Egypt as their example of God's response to people in need. Perhaps what comes to mind is the strength and persistence that a friend showed in the face of adversity, and we credit God with supporting that person in the struggle. We might hold up the example of a saint in our tradition who contended with similar difficulties. Saint Hildegard of Bingen suffered chronic illness and yet found the strength to write beautiful music that endures well beyond the twelfth century in which it was composed. Twentieth-century Catholic Henri Nouwen disclosed his confusion upon losing a clear sense of his vocational calling and the searching that led him to a renewed understanding of his purpose and work. Elizabeth Cady Stanton, Jarena Lee, and Martin Luther King Jr. met the challenges of gender and race segregation with the belief that God would overcome these injustices and lived to see some social movement in these areas. We pull these kinds of examples to the forefront of our minds in prayers of lament so that we will feel less isolated in our suffering and more aware of God's faithfulness throughout human history.

Laments also include words explicitly seeking divine help for that which troubles us. In the first verse of Psalm 60, the psalmist (who is identified as King David) wrote, "O God, you have rejected us, broken our defenses; you have been angry; now restore us!" Under siege by the armies of Edom, the king wastes no time telling God what is needed to turn the situation around. He repeats his requests for help in verses 5 ("Give victory with your right hand, and answer us, so that those whom you love may be rescued") and 11 ("O grant us help against the foe, for human help is worthless"). Do we not have similar desires when we feel overwhelmed by unrealistic demands, personal tragedy, or social instability? Perhaps even more to the point for children and adults contending with spiteful comments, insensitive teasing or braggarts are the words of the third and fourth verses of Psalm 12: "May the Lord cut off all flattering lips, the tongue that makes great boasts, those who say, 'With our tongues we will prevail; our lips are our own—who is our master?'" We need not use the psalmists' exact words in our own laments, but we can pattern our statements about our anger and frustration with life's injustices on the candor of the biblical lamentations rather than covering over our true feelings with platitudes that suggest we are untouched emotionally by our sufferings.

The final component of a lament is a statement praising God for what has been and will be done to resolve the crisis we are experiencing. How is God providing people and other resources to support us in our time of trouble? What comfort have we found in recalling our connections with those who have gone before us in faithfulness? What new gifts and abilities have we discovered in ourselves (or

Personal and Corporate Laments

Because prayers of lament are not as familiar as some other types of praying, exploring some biblical laments (on our own or with our children) can help us learn to create our own. The Hebrew Bible psalms are a rich source of laments; following are exercises related to two psalms, Psalm 13 (a personal lament) and Psalm 80 (a corporate prayer).

PSALM 13: MODEL OF A PERSONAL LAMENT
Read Psalm 13 aloud. Notice how and where the five elements of a typical personal lament are expressed in this short prayer:

1. Invocation or address to God—verses 1 and 3
2. Complaint—verses 1–4
3. Expression of confidence or trust—verse 5
4. Petition or supplication—verse 3
5. Expression of praise or vow to praise—verse 6

Think about the following questions (or discuss them with your children):

Are there any expressions of lament in this psalm with which you identify?
In what ways does this psalm express your trust and confidence in God?

PSALM 80: MODEL OF A CORPORATE LAMENT
Corporate laments typically have six elements because they divide the "expression of confidence or trust" into two components: remembering God's past actions and words of

REAL KIDS, REAL FAITH

affirmation. Read Psalm 80 aloud, and see if you can identify places where each of the six elements are represented. Then create your own brief corporate lament on the same theme as Psalm 80, using the following questions to guide you:

What are the things that threaten the health and well-being of your family? Or ask younger children, "What things are you afraid will hurt our family?" (These things are the content of your complaint.)

How do you want to address God, given these threats? To younger children: "What would be a good name to call God if we think God can help us with this problem?" (This is the invocation.)

What stories about God's actions in the past relate to these concerns? Children: "Can you think of any stories from the Bible in which God dealt with a problem like this before?" (This is the first half of the expression of confidence, in which you remember God's past actions.)

What can you affirm about God because of these stories or your past experiences as a family? Children: "How did God deal with the problem in these stories?" (These are the words of affirmation that make up the second half of the expression of confidence.)

What do you want God to do about these threats or problems? Children can answer this question as well as adults. (These are your petitions.)

What response to God's future actions will you make now out of trust? Children: "If you really believe God will help, how are you going to act?" (This is your expression of praise.)

If you haven't created your corporate lament as a family activity, you might want to invite other members of your family to join you in praying the lament together.

discovered we need to cultivate) through our ordeal? What aspects of God's nature bring us comfort and hope? These are the questions that help us and our children draw on the spiritual resources of our life with God.

Sometimes we may need to sit in silence with God to find these points of praise; indeed, we may have to do the same to recall the promises of God's responsive love that make up the middle component of a lament. But it is important to note that laments both complain (sometimes vociferously!) to and about God *and* affirm God's steadfast love and mercy. If we dwell only in the mode of complaint, we will soon fall into despair and cynicism, and eventually we will see no reason for continued communication with God. But equally dangerous for our ongoing spiritual formation is our propensity to communicate with God only in the mode of affirming God's will and God's love. This withholds from God the particular struggles and strains of our daily quest to live a faithful life in an imperfect world where, as Rabbi Harold Kushner has put it, "bad things happen to good people." Too often we fear that God will punish us if we appear to challenge God's will or make demands. Honest engagement with the God who forms us in faith requires that we trust God to receive our frustration and demands for justice with the same compassionate love we presume fuels God's interest in us in the first place.

Laments can be personal or communal. Approximately 45 of the 150 biblical psalms are personal laments; another 20 are corporate pleas for help and deliverance. Families can lament together the injustices they experience or see in the world around them. As adults guide children through the steps of a family lament, they model a way of coping with life's difficulties and set-backs that focuses on more than just the worrisome aspect of a situation or event. Prayers of lament treat with respect both the very real challenges of living faithfully and the hopeful history of such faithfulness on the part of God and humans throughout the centuries. Children need permission both to see and feel what is wrong with the world and to imagine and believe in change that will address those problems. Otherwise, they fall prey to the same stress-induced illnesses and social distress that adults who feel beleaguered and powerless experience. The rising incidence of teen suicide and a growing childhood mental health treatment industry suggest, in part, that anxiety, depression, and distress are real problems among children. Learning to lament could be one means by which children discover that with God, they are no longer alone or powerless.

ADDITIONAL BIBLICAL FORMS OF PRAYER

The scriptures of the Jewish and Christian traditions offer us several models of people praying in forms other than silence or laments. For biblical people, the focus of their spoken prayers generally reflected their circumstances and how they perceived God in relationship to their situation. They would offer prayers of praise, confession, petition, intercession, and thanksgiving, depending on their needs and on the state of their relationship with God at a particular time. They might engage in prayer as a means of naming and affirming their desire for a disciplined spiritual life—a life of discipleship—or to put into words the commitments they believed themselves bound to honor in light of God's actions in the world. Their prayers can become our prayers and our children's prayers, either through direct adoption of their words (when that seems appropriate) or the use of our own words to speak with God about similar celebrations and concerns.

Prayers of Praise

Famous with children for his slingshot ability and harp playing, King David provides an unconventional model for prayers of praise in his exuberant celebration of God's presence among the Israelites. He gathered the people around him and the Ark of the Covenant (the symbol of God's presence) and began to dance and shout with joy. Musicians threw in a trumpet fanfare, resulting (at least to my imagination) in a carnival-like atmosphere of unrestrained and joyous praise. The biblical text (2 Samuel 6:12–16) says that David's wife was actually rather taken aback by her husband's lack of decorum. I like to think that David was allowing his true delight in who God is and what God had been doing in his life and community to spill out in much the same way a young child dances for joy when something good happens. We can encourage our children to express their delight in God's creation and God's goodness with words and bodily expressions of praise. Singing hymns of praise from our tradition's songbooks, creating shouts and cheers (with appropriate jumping up and down if desired), and shouting "alleluia" or "hurray, God" when they see something great that God is doing in the world are all ways children can exuberantly praise God. Quieter forms of praise include saying, "Praise God" to oneself or listing reasons for praising God with the rest of the family as part of a mealtime prayer.

Prayers of Confession and Forgiveness

"Screwing up," as my children like to call it, is something human beings are pretty good at doing. It is difficult to live well in relationship with one another all day, every day. It is even more difficult to let every moment of our days be guided and directed by the values and commitments that our spiritual journeys are leading us to embrace. Biblical people also struggled with misshapen relationships and misplaced loyalties. They turned to God to confess their errors and seek divine forgiveness as a first step toward righting what they had done wrong. They believed that strength for repairing what had become broken came from God.

Here, too, David provides a model for praying. After being confronted about an affair in which he had also arranged to have the woman's husband killed in battle, he had much wrongdoing to confess. His prayer seeking God's forgiveness is Psalm 51.

> Create in me a clean heart, O God,
>   and put a new and right spirit within me.
> Do not cast me away from your presence,
>   and do not take your holy spirit from me.
> Restore to me the joy of your salvation,
>   and sustain in me a willing spirit.

> Then I will teach transgressors your ways,
>   and sinners will return to you.
> PSALM 51:10–13

David's plea is essentially for the opportunity to start anew, but with a difference: with God's help, he will focus more attention on the ways of God—so much attention, in fact, that he will be able to teach those ways to others. Our own transgressions may not seem as horrible as David's were, yet imagine how differently we might lead our lives if we actively sought to learn from our mistakes sufficiently well that we could share what we have learned with others. Imagine helping our children name their wrongdoing and then identify how they can learn a better way so well that others might learn from their example. This process can be as simple as asking children to share one or two mistakes they have made recently, brainstorming together about how they might have acted differently, and then asking God's forgiveness and help in making the change. We are often intrigued by people who have overcome great adversity to succeed in life. Our family prayers of confession and forgiveness help us recognize the spiritual power that infuses such changes, even when they are on a much more modest scale.

Prayers of Supplication or Petition

The pattern of prayer into which we fall most often is that of asking God to do things for us. God invites us to share our concerns about getting our basic needs met, similar to the way young children pen a wish list to Santa Claus. We've already seen how this way of petitioning God for something is an aspect of lament. Paul, an early Christian teacher, wrote to his followers, "Do not worry about anything, but in everything by prayer and supplication with thanksgiving let your requests be made known to God" (Philippians 4:6).

The Jewish prophet Ezra tells the story of petitioning God for a safe journey on which he and a band of Israelites returned to their homeland from exile in Babylon (Ezra 8:21–23). Prayers of petition are closely tied to letting go of worry. We can encourage our children to ask God to provide for their needs rather than worry about whether their needs will be met. When my daughter was having difficulty sleeping, I suggested she ask God to give her a good night's rest. She had become so worried she would wake up during the night that she had trouble falling asleep each evening because she felt responsible for making herself sleep well. Now that she has entrusted the quality of her sleep to God, she rests easier. Many traditional bedtime prayers for children use this same petition.

Prayers of Intercession

We pray not only for the provision of our basic needs; we also intercede with God on behalf of the well-being of others. Prayers of intercession attend to an ever-widening circle of our neighbors in the world. The Jewish prophet Nehemiah, who followed Ezra as a leader of the Israelites who had come out of exile, heard of the plight of some survivors and immediately he "sat down and wept, and mourned for days, fasting and praying before the God of heaven" on their behalf (Nehemiah 1:4). His prayer focused on the most inward circle of his neighbors, his immediate community. Encouraging our children to pray for the members of their immediate and extended family imitates Nehemiah's prayer. We can do this by naming family members during family prayer times as well as at more impromptu moments, such as after the receipt of a letter or phone call that reminds us of their needs.

Other, wider circles of intercessory prayer are for the suffering and troubled, our local community, the world, and our faith tradition's communities throughout the world. When my family notices a broken-down car or an accident on the side of the road, we pray for the people involved because they may be suffering and they are certainly experiencing trouble. Families can also pray for the events they see and hear about in the news. Sometimes such events may shock us into wordlessness; then our prayers of intercession may be more tears and silence than spoken words. It can be enough to name what seems in need of God's attention in the same manner as the stereotypical children's bedtime litany of people and things for God to "bless." When I work with groups of children, we sometimes create paper chains in which each link contains the name of someone or something in need of intercession. This creates a tangible sign of all that we are entrusting to God's care through our prayers.

Prayers of Thanksgiving

Learning to say "please" and "thank you" is a basic component of growing up. Prayers of petition are akin to the former, and prayers of thanksgiving pick up on the latter. When we teach our children to give thanks to God, we are reminding them to acknowledge the spiritual source of their being and well-being. Many families have developed a tradition around the cultural holiday of Thanksgiving in which everyone names something for which they are thankful as part of the celebratory meal. A variation on this theme is to name something for which we are thankful about each person at the table. It is a small step from such a cultural ritual to a regular practice of offering God thanks for the many good things we enjoy in life.

The biblical woman, Hannah, was so delighted to have a son after years of infertility that her exultant prayer of thanksgiving has a special place in Jewish and Christian scriptures as the Song of Hannah (1 Samuel 2:1–10). In it, she celebrates not only her own good fortune but the ways in which God can turn the expectations of the world upside down. Her acclamation that "those who were full have hired themselves out for bread, but those who were hungry are fat with spoil" reminds us of something else we need to teach our children about prayers of thanksgiving: they are not meant to underscore with God how much we deserve all the things we have. Rather, they are an acknowledgment that the one who created the universe and all that is has provided enough for all, and we are thankful for our portion. The simple question, "What do we have to thank God for today?" can prompt children to join us in prayers of thanksgiving.

Prayers of Discipleship

It is because we sometimes have more than our portion that prayers of discipleship go well with prayers of thanksgiving. In the Christian scriptures (Matthew 6:9–13), it is recorded that Jesus taught his disciples to pray,

> Our Father in heaven, hallowed be your name.
> Your kingdom come. Your will be done, on earth as it is in heaven.
> Give us this day our daily bread.
> And forgive us our debts, as we also have forgiven our debtors.
> And do not bring us to the time of trial, but rescue us from the evil one.

These words orient those who pray toward God's ways and call attention to their responsibility to relate to others as they would have God relate to them. Can we honestly ask God to provide for our daily needs and then set about hoarding material goods for ourselves? Not if we want to be consistent in our words and actions. Prayers of discipleship function to remind us of the relational quality of God's presence and our attempts to embody that presence in our own lives.

Christianity is not the only faith tradition to call its followers to discipleship. The Muslim Al-Fatiha or Exordium is similar to the Lord's Prayer. Printed on the opening page of the Koran and frequently recited, it says,

> In the Name of God the Compassionate, the Merciful.
> Praise be to God, Lord of the Universe,
> The Compassionate, the Merciful,
> Sovereign of the Day of Judgment!
> You alone we worship, and to You alone we turn for help.
> Guide us to the straight path,
> The path of those whom You have favored,
> Not of those who have incurred Your wrath,
> Nor of those who have gone astray.

Imagine praying such powerful words several times a day! Like Muslim children and adults, we need to remind ourselves and our children that they should worship only God, petition God for help, and seek to follow the example of the faithful who have gone before them. We need to embrace the prayers of our tradition, such as the Lord's Prayer, that offer guidance for our spiritual journey. Not only can we pray this prayer with our children regularly, we can take time to talk together about what we think each part of the prayer means. We might try having family members put the Lord's Prayer in their own words once in a while. We can also encourage children to construct their own prayers of discipleship in which they name what they believe about God and the spiritual life and commit themselves to live according to those beliefs. Make a simple table together that has a column for your family's beliefs about God and spiritual living and a column for each person, noting how he or she will try to live a faithful

---

Biblical Prayer Forms

Although not an exhaustive list, the seven biblical forms of spoken prayer described in this chapter can help your family learn how to engage in a rich and diverse prayer life in combination with contemplation and meditation. This quick primer summarized the types in a handy list that lets you keep track of which forms are becoming part of your family's regular routine and which are not receiving much time and attention. Use this list to help you create a good working balance.

Prayer Form	Practiced This Week?
Lament (trusting enough to complain)	
Praise (delighting in God and God's creation)	
Confession-Forgiveness (seeking restoration)	
Petition (asking for basic needs)	
Intercession (seeking well-being of others)	
Thanksgiving (showing appreciation)	
Discipleship (attending to God's guidance)	

life in relation to those beliefs. If your family believes that God cares for the poor and wants us to do the same, each person would think of a way to help God care for the poor and write that idea in his or her column. Then the whole family would ask God to support the desires of each to live out his or her commitment faithfully.

PRAYER AS A LIFELONG CONVERSATION WITH GOD

In silence and in speaking, prayer is a conversation with God that nurtures and supports our spiritual lives. As Lois Rock says in her children's book, *A First Look: Prayer,* "Prayer is a way of making friends with God." Sometimes we tell God about our hopes, fears, needs, beliefs, struggles, gifts, and general state of being. Other times we listen for God's side of the story, knowing that God's words may come in many forms. If we are sitting in silence, they may enter our awareness as a thought or idea that persistently demands our attention. They may sink into our being more intuitively through our contemplation on the words, artwork, or music of others. We may read a passage from our tradition's sacred texts and realize that those words speak to our situation. They may even be carried to us in the words or deeds of another person, with or without that person's awareness of speaking for God. However God's words come to us, they do not come once and fade away into unremitting silence. Prayer draws us and our children ever closer into intimate relationship with the divine. It is a lifelong conversation with a lifelong spiritual friend.

Chapter 6

SUPPORTING CHILDREN AS THEY GROW IN SPIRITUAL AWARENESS

Young children commonly engage the world with a sense of wonder and awe. Ordinary events in their lives can elicit expressions of pleasure, as in the toddler's delighted "Hi!" when a working parent comes home each evening. Movement through the park or the mall proceeds slowly because they want to stop and look at everything along the way. Even older children embrace the world with an eye to new discoveries. My eight-year-old son just realized that our front hallway makes a great "slip and slide" if he puts on his snow pants and gloves and dives toward the back door. The possibility never occurred to me, and I can't say that I'm entirely happy that it occurred to him, either! But it does demonstrate an openness to possibilities, to being amazed by what the world offers and what one can do with those offerings.

Negative experiences may also generate responses of curiosity and amazement. The same child who dives down hallways watched with fascination and a few grimaces of pain while the surgeon removed a metal pin from his elbow, placed there because of a mishap unrelated to his recent sliding escapades. He wanted to see his X-rays and learn all about how the stitches under his skin would dissolve on their own. His inquisitiveness is typical of children his age, although not all eight-year-olds handle injury and its aftermath with such aplomb. The younger child, who, with thumb tucked in her mouth, gazes steadily at a worrisome dog on the other side of a fence, evidences a similar fascination in the context of a negative experience. She is taking in an aspect of the world, and her encounter with the dog is shaping her perceptions of herself, animals, and safety.

Stories, too, generate wonder. My daughter's favorite book as a one-year-old was Audrey and Don Wood's *The Little Mouse, The Red Ripe Strawberry, and The Big Hungry Bear*. Her eyes would get as big as the central character's eyes when we read about how the little mouse was trying to protect his juicy strawberry (through disguises and barriers) from the unseen menace of the bear. The eventual resolution of the dilemma, in which the mouse shares his treat with the still unrevealed bear, had her clapping her hands in amazement. My daughter remains so enamored with this story and its characters that she rushed out to get the author's only sequel (*Merry Christmas, Big Hungry Bear*) when it was published this year, even though she is now eleven. It is no coincidence that she continues to wrestle with how to make meaning in the face of fears about others and the unknown, just as the mouse depicted in these books does in every reading.

Returning parents, physical feats, broken bones, and spellbinding books are all contexts and content for spiritual experiences. Yet conscious spiritual reflection on the causes or reasons for a wondrous or troublesome experience is a learned response. Spiritual awareness, in contrast with spiritual experience, has to be activated or it may remain dormant for long periods, even most of a lifetime. We can participate in particular experiences or hear certain stories and even develop uncritical responses to those experiences and stories as a matter of course. But critical and sustained spiritual reflection on the meaning of our experiences and our culture's stories for our lives depends on the acknowledgment and development of a reflective process, the acquisition of religious information that supports meaning making, and the stirring of our imaginations.

REFLECTIVE PROCESSES

Children use their minds to sort and categorize data from their encounters with their environment. A newborn baby uses the sense of smell to associate the scent of his mother with the availability of food, then he roots to suckle. A five-year-old painstakingly sounds out a word in order to connect the individual letters she has learned into her newly developing comprehension of written communication. A nine-year-old constructs bar graphs and pie charts in science class to help him draw conclusions about the data from his experiments. A fifteen-year-old writes a research paper analyzing various newspaper articles on whether the country should go to war and develops her own arguable position. Developmental delays may mean that some children reflect in ways that are inconsistent with their chronological age, but unless a child has severe brain damage, he or she is a rational (thinking) person from birth.

However, children can only sort data according to the categories and concepts they have available to them at any particular time. The newborn who seeks out his mother for milk is using a simple form of associative reasoning based on his senses and limited life experience. The five-year-old sounds out her words by applying the phonics lessons provided by her parents or teachers. The nine-year-old scientist uses the assessment frameworks of elementary science rather than college-level chemistry, which limits the way he presents his data and the conclusions he draws. The high school paper-writer brings the requirements of the assignment and the limits or expansiveness of her own ethical development to her work. None of these children will reflect on the spiritual significance of their experiences or ideas if the adults in their lives do not provide the spiritual categories and concepts of the family's faith tradition for use in structuring their understanding. The spiritual world that we create for our children to inhabit, with its content of religious stories, language, and prayer, enables our children to think spiritually. It sets the stage for the cultivation of spiritual awareness.

Supporting Children as They Grow in Spiritual Awareness

DEVELOPMENTALLY SENSITIVE AWARENESS

Adults who wish to encourage spiritual reflection by children can do that best by affirming that children are capable of understanding religious concepts and practices on their own developmental level and that their understandings, although different from those of adults, are valuable. As Catholic theologian Karl Rahner has stated, "We conceive of an innate spiritual capacity in childhood, but recognize that this may focus in particular ways and take different and changing forms as the child's other capacities develop." Spiritual awareness, then, is developmentally sensitive, which means we need to tailor our expectations of children's spiritual reflection to their age and stage of psychosocial development.

Consider the implications of this developmental sensitivity for a two-year-old child's interpretations of religious stories. Older toddlers are bound by what Jean Piaget, a developmental psychologist, identified as "irreversibility." They observe objects and individuals in particular moments and do not interpret what they see in light of past states or actions. Piaget conducted a series of experiments in which young children were presented with two identical glasses (labeled A and B) filled with equal amounts of water. The children then were shown a taller and narrower glass (labeled C) and asked if the water amounts would remain the same if the water from glass A were poured into glass C and then glasses B and C were compared. Based on their observations of glasses A and B, the children believed the water amounts would be the same. However, when they actually saw the water in glass C, they believed that glass C contained more water than glass B because the water level in glass C was higher than that of glass B. Despite their earlier observation of glasses A and B and their earlier certainty that the amounts of water were equal, their last observation of two different water levels dominated their interpretation. They could not reason backward from what they were seeing to what they observed before and logically alter their visual perception with foreknowledge.

This type of irreversible thinking actually assists two-year-olds in making sense of religious narratives because older toddlers are un-

Age-Related Concepts of God

Children's perceptions of God shift as they gain new and different developmental capabilities. Changes in their physical strength and endurance recast their sense of God's power. More expansive social experience allows for different kinds of reflection on how God interacts with the world. Changing cognitive abilities also affect critical reflection conclusions. The typical age-related unfolding of such changes allows us to make the following generalizations about what children know about God:

Birth to three years God is a real person who lives in a place called heaven or at one's house of worship. God provides comfort (like a blankie) and cares for one like a parent.

Three to eight years God is great in ways similar to superheroes. God watches people all year round like Santa Claus to decide who to reward and who to punish. God acts like a magician, making things happen that can't be explained. God is concerned with reciprocal fairness.

Nine to twelve years God is involved in the various systems (ecological, social, political) that shape one's world. God is like a friend who takes a personal interest in one's activities. Who God is and how God works are puzzles to be investigated.

Teens God is a confidant, guide, and counselor. God is especially concerned with one's personal moral behavior. God seems to operate behind the scenes in social systems, but it is hard to know what is God's activity and what is human activity.

concerned with the moral dilemmas embedded in many religious texts. They appreciate the story of Noah and the ark because all the animals are safe from the flood. Young children do not struggle to resolve, as adults do, the logical tension between a theological doctrine

Supporting Children as They Grow in Spiritual Awareness

of God's grace and the narrative claim that God once destroyed most of the world because of sin. Instead, they interpret religious texts through the lens of their own egocentric concerns and in terms of their own actions and feelings. If they are afraid of thunderstorms, they assume that the animals were afraid also and that Noah, who is presumed to be like the adults in their social world, had the job of providing comfort and reassurance. If they have experienced a boat ride, they presume that the population of the ark had the same experience they did. Their intuitive logical perspective encourages them to create simple mental pictures of stories that coordinate with their simple mental images of their own experiences.

With very young children, parents can name aloud the simple intuitive interpretations their toddlers and preschoolers are inclined to make and thus reinforce their children's process of making sense of their world. Such positive reinforcement encourages toddlers to repeat the process in other situations, much as acknowledging a child's first attempts to dress himself encourages further engagement in dressing. We can tell the story of Noah and then talk with our young children about it. Linking statements like "the animals were afraid of the rain" and "Noah took care of the animals for God" associates the animals' experience with that of the child and provides religious language for how such fears are addressed by God. Although the child is not yet capable of consciously stating the analogy between herself and the animals, she experiences the connection (because of her developmentally egocentric view that everything is about her) and intuitively operates with it as a guide to her own way of being in the world.

Story commentaries and other statements such as this also help a young child develop a concept of God that makes sense. An infant or toddler who has heard a parent say each night at bedtime, "God is watching over you while you sleep," likely will develop a concept of God as someone close by who is waiting to care for her, just as she has experienced the parent as someone in a nearby room prepared to do the same. That God's attention may be mediated through the actions of loving adult caregivers rather than offered directly by a particular person named God does not trouble the toddler. She presumes that someone named God could indeed step in to provide care if another person does not do so. In the absence of a concrete and soothing adult presence, the toddler can invoke the idea of God as a means of reassurance and self-soothing, much as she might call to mind the image of a primary caregiver.

GOD TALK WITH PRESCHOOL AND EARLY ELEMENTARY CHILDREN

Young children who have learned to converse in sentences have also gained reasoning abilities that expand the ways in which they engage religious ideas. For instance, they can organize their thoughts and hold a conversation with an adult about a religious concept, whereas younger children mostly echo the statements of adults. John Hull, a British professor of religious education, capitalized on this conversational ability in order to study the ways in which children ages three through eight think and talk about God. The data for his study came from exchanges (most of them spontaneous) he had with his own children. One conversation explores a common theme of children's imaginative thinking about God: the comparison of God to a superhero. Hull asks two of his children, "Who can jump higher then, God or Superman?" Both the five-year-old and the six-and-a-half-year-old identify God as the better jumper. Hull asks, "But can God jump? What would happen if he jumped?" The older child excitedly responds, "He'd jump into himself. He's already there. He's everywhere. He doesn't need to jump." Hull then asks whether God or Superman is faster. The same child notes that Superman can go around the earth very fast, but God's "there already."

Hull's example points to the way in which preschool and early elementary children draw on both social and religious frameworks to sort out who God is and how God works. The idea that God has superhero powers intrigues both of Hull's children, and then the older child realizes that something else he has been taught about God complicates the idea. God is omnipresent, or present everywhere. So God can't act quite the same as a superhero. As Hull points out in his com-

Supporting Children as They Grow in Spiritual Awareness

mentary on this example, the five-year-old doesn't yet understand the distinction made by the older sibling. But at six-and-a-half, the other child has grasped a basic tenet of several faith traditions: that God is inherently different from any other thing, in this case because God is omnipresent.

Sometimes, as in the case just described, it is the recollection of a bit of religious information (God's omnipresence) in relation to a non-religious framework (the exploits of superheroes) that brings a child to fuller spiritual awareness. At other times, the application of a social framework functions to help a child make sense of a piece of religious information. When the eight-year-old I mentioned in Chapter Three explained the crucifixion of Jesus in terms of people not using their words and needing to take a time out, she was drawing on a behavioral norm often repeated to elementary children in North American homes and schools. She discerned in the Christian passion narrative a problem akin to her own experience and applied the social explanation she deemed most fitting. Her social awareness of the threat that anger can pose to relationships deepened her spiritual awareness of the tension between good and evil in the central story of her faith tradition. Adults support such expressions of spiritual awareness when we encourage God-talk that is experimental rather than definitional, when we honor interpretations that express connections between faith stories and children's lives, even though these expressions may or may not conform fully to the traditional doctrines of our religious tradition.

Spiritual Reflection and Nine- to Twelve-Year-Olds

The negotiations children make between their understandings of social systems and their apprehension of the spiritual life continue in the older elementary and early middle school years. Rabbi Harold Kushner, quoting another Jewish thinker, Mordecai Kaplan, contends that there are "two not-so-simple steps" involved in helping children explore their questions about God: "(1) the ability to answer the ques-

Children and Sacred Scriptures

Just as children's perceptions and interpretations of God change over time, their understanding of a tradition's sacred scriptures shifts as well. Infants and young toddlers begin to acquire a sense of the special nature of a religious text if they witness adults treating a book with reverence and hear a particular book identified as important. By the time a child is three, he or she can readily identify a Bible as a book that's different from other storybooks. But it is not until school-age, when the ability to read and understand books typically develops, that further critical awareness of the nature of sacred scriptures also develops.

Younger elementary children can recognize that sacred texts were written by a variety of people living at different times and in different places. They can understand the system of books, chapters, and verses that characterizes most scriptural texts and use this system to find the location of particular stories or sayings. They can explain some of the ways in which the culture of the religious text is different from their own culture, and they may begin to recognize different genres of writing (poetry, rule codes, first- and third-person narratives, and so on) contained within the scriptures.

Older elementary children begin to understand the basic chronology of stories within sacred texts and recognize finer distinctions in the literary genres used. They are able to use a variety of secondary resources (for example, commentaries, concordances, religious dictionaries, maps of ancient lands) to help them interpret what they read. They are also capable of identifying significant themes that run throughout scriptural texts as they cultivate the skill of interpreting ideas represented in different ways in a variety of stories.

tion to the satisfaction of an adult, and (2) the ability to adapt that answer to a child's mind in accordance with his [or her] age." Kushner's point is that our own thinking about religious concepts helps us provide our children with references for their reflections. Older elementary and middle school children are particularly interested in such reference points because of their burgeoning interest in scientific reasoning. As they learn about research procedures in their school work, they apply similar strategies to their inquiries about spiritual matters. They solicit parental perspectives, read books (if they are readily available), and compare notes on what they are finding out about God.

Children this age readily notice inconsistencies between religious explanations and scientific ones and ask for clarification. When my children were studying the big bang theory in science class, they came home asking questions about how this theory related to the creation stories they were hearing in Sunday school. We talked about the difference between literal and metaphorical truth, looking into the reasons behind each claim and asking ourselves if and how they could both be true. Because my children had developed the cognitive ability to imagine more than one plausible explanation for the same event, we could explore why people might choose to give one explanation more weight than another in particular circumstances, without that preference negating the possible truth of the other explanations.

The older children grow, the more we can encourage them to acknowledge and wrestle with multiple perspectives. Any child over the age of three or four has the cognitive and emotional ability to recognize difference, but the dominant egocentrism of young children interferes with their ability to look at something from another person's point of view. It is not until age ten or so that a child's reasoning ability and social experiences lend themselves to sustained reflection on and complex judgments about the veracity of a variety of perspectives. Sharing with them our own reflections on the spiritual life and inviting them to reflect with one another as well draws them into conversation with people who experience God in similar and different ways. They discover that the explanations they have for how God works in the world are sometimes affirmed by their friends and sometimes challenged. They realize that the ideas their friends have about forgiveness answer some of their questions and not others. They ideally interact with a religious community that welcomes their questioning and their ongoing exploration of the provisional answers they find.

THE IMPORTANCE OF QUESTIONING

Edith Bajema, an active layperson in the Christian Reformed tradition, finds in both the Hebrew scriptures and in Jesus' teachings a spiritual practice of asking questions and receiving answers. She credits children with a capacity for thoughtful inquisitiveness that should elicit from adults equally thoughtful responses along the lines of the model of Jewish rabbinic debate. Rather than being too busy to answer children's questions (like the adults in Marc Gellman's story, "Does God Have a Big Toe?" described in Chapter Three), our job as parents and caregivers of children is to listen to their questions and find time to talk about possible answers. We may not be able to drop whatever we are doing when a question arises, and we shouldn't feel compelled to do so when we do not have that freedom. But we can acknowledge the question and demonstrate our interest in further conversation at a more convenient time, which we specifically designate and then create as promised.

Like John Hull with his superhero query, we can also be the ones who pose intriguing questions for our children to explore. When I took my younger children to the American Girl Tea Room a few years ago, there was a box in the center of our table that contained cards with questions. The cards asked such things as, "What do you want to be doing in five years?" and "If you could live on a different planet, which one would it be?" We spent nearly the entire tea time drawing cards and sharing our answers with one another. Imagine a box full of spiritual question cards: "How do you think God feels about war?" "What would Jesus do on Christmas?" "Is God a magician?" "What do you think God is like?" "Where would Moses sit if he came to eat lunch at your school?"

The Youth and Family Institute, an Evangelical Lutheran Church in America organization in Minneapolis, has actually created

Children's Religious Questions

Elizabeth Caldwell, in *Making a Home for Faith,* suggests that children's religious questions fall into four categories. The following examples of each type of question may help you recognize the sorts of questions your own children are asking.

1. *Informational*—questions that have factual or demonstrable answers, such as "When did Queen Esther live?" or "What did Moses do when he saw the burning bush?"
2. *Analytical*—questions that require an interpretation of meaning, such as "Why wouldn't Pharaoh let the Israelites leave Egypt?" or "Why was Jesus killed?"
3. *Experiential*—questions that arise out of a child's observations and reflections, such as "Why did my friend get cancer?" or "Why do we kneel when we pray?"
4. *Wondering*—questions pertaining to the mystery of God, such as "What does God look like?" or "How does God talk to people?"

The first two types of questions are generally easier for adults to handle because we can look up the answers to informational questions with our children or walk through a reasoned response to analytical queries. Experiential and wondering questions may push us to admit what we do not know ourselves and, if we're willing, invite us to ponder alongside our children the deep concerns of a spiritually attuned life.

a set of such questions. Called "Faith Talk with Children," this cloth wallet containing ninety-six question cards is designed for families to use over dinner, in the car, or anywhere children and adults make time to talk with one another. Some of the questions invite children and adults to remember something that happened in their past, such as a time they "felt close to God." Others focus on helping children and adults become more faithful: "What are you really good at? How could you use this skill to help God?" There is a subset of questions that pick up on religious ideas that children are likely to wonder about and asks them (and their adult caregivers) to respond imaginatively: "If you were an angel, what would you like to do?" Another subset attends to the development of a spiritual disposition: "If God came to your house, how would you say hello?" "Faith Talk" is designed for Christian families, but three-quarters of the cards phrase their questions in religious language (as in the examples given) that is common to Jewish and Muslim spirituality as well.

AWARENESS THROUGH ARTISTIC REFLECTIONS

We need not limit our spiritual explorations with children to spoken conversations. Spiritual awareness is also awakened through other forms of expression. Meditating on artwork, music, or poetry (as discussed in the preceding chapter) invites us into other peoples' perspectives and lets other parts of our brain work on the mystery of God and God's relationship with us. Engaging in artistic work also helps us make new spiritual discoveries.

Noted child psychiatrist Robert Coles talks about the amazingly powerful ways that children's artwork helps them identify and convey what they believe about God. In response to Coles's question, "Where does God live?" children ages eight to twelve (plus one four-year-old) painted or drew pictures of what they imagine as God's dwelling place. Coles then published a small collection of these pictures, accompanied by the artists' comments on their images. Some children drew pictures of God on a mountaintop or a throne. One has a ladder ascending into a cloud. An eight-year-old painted God as a figure beside him in his house, set against a bright blue sky, then told Coles, "God lives in Heaven and in my house."

I shared Coles's book, *In God's House,* with a group of children in my congregation, then asked them to paint their own pictures of

God's house. Their images ranged from a depiction of the solar system to a likeness of the church building. The enthusiasm with which they (and the children in Coles's study) accepted the assignment suggests that children are already thinking about such questions. When parents or caregivers ask them to make their thoughts known, they have an opportunity to test their interpretations with persons they trust. If their adult questioners also create images to share or offer them images from their religious tradition as comparable or alternative ideas, then children's spiritual lives are enriched by their participation in a communal artistic discourse of interpretation similar to the spoken exchanges described earlier.

SPIRITUAL AWARENESS AND TEENAGERS

Adolescents, by virtue of their longer life experience and schooling, are even more aware of the multiplicity of perspectives available for interpreting personal experiences. Because they have often been exposed to cultural and educational systems that downplay spirituality or trivialize it as emotionality, they can be quite skeptical of spiritual experience and religious claims. They also pay close attention to whether persons who say they are spiritual actually live out the commitments of their spirituality. Their questions for spiritual reflection run the gamut from mild curiosity (What's the difference between the Amish and the Mennonites?) to hostile demands (How can anyone believe in God after 9/11?). They are not always patient with adult attempts to wave aside hard questions with placating phrases like "We cannot know the mind of God" or "God will explain everything when we get to heaven."

A group of fifteen adolescent girls and I were talking about the Christian story of Thomas, the disciple who was skeptical about Christ's resurrection. As part of our discussion, I offered the girls the opportunity to write their own questions anonymously on note cards so that we could explore them together. Their concerns included these:

Is heaven for people with all religions? Or just for those that are Catholic/Christian?

Why was God so devoted to the world?

I learned being gay is a sin; is it? Will you go to hell?

Did the forbidden fruit (in the Garden of Eden) stand for sex?

Why are people in places like Kosovo so mean to each other?

Why must babies and young children die when mothers and fathers pray so hard for help?

When people commit suicide do they go to hell?

How can we ask God for help when we are in trouble?

Some of their questions (who goes to heaven or hell, what is meant by "forbidden fruit") focused on whether particular religious ideas they had heard were true. Other queries (God's devotion, human hatred, children dying) expressed confusion and curiosity about the nature of God and God's power in relation to the world. A few questions, such as what to do when in trouble, focused on how they might be in relationship with God.

Adults can expect teens to wonder about these sorts of issues in terms of both the theoretical and practical implications of any particular conclusion. The girl who asked whether persons who commit suicide go to hell had a particular friend who had died in mind. She had also attempted suicide once herself. Underlying her question about suicide and hell were other questions about her own worthiness as a spiritual being loved by God. Not every query adolescents pose is fraught with life-and-death significance, but each question represents an attempt to construct a meaningful spiritual framework within which to live a life without hypocrisy.

PREPARING OURSELVES FOR QUESTIONS

Children of all ages typically turn first to their parents with their questions about spirituality. The good news for us parents is that we need not be expert answerers in order to nurture our children's spiritual awareness. Instead, we bring our own inquisitiveness to bear, reading books that explore our faith tradition, talking with other adults about the issues our children raise, and researching with our children possible answers to their questions and to ours. Helen Oppenheimer, an Anglican Christian, became so caught up in imagining the kinds of questions her grandchildren would want to explore with her and their parents someday that she wrote a book titled *Helping Children Find God,* for Christian adults looking for a starting place of their own. Jewish Lights Publishing has a fourteen-volume series, *The Way Into. . .,* of short books introducing Jewish beliefs and practices to nonscholars like interfaith parents. For those who would rather start with a single accessible reference book on the Jewish faith, the publishing house also has produced Arthur Green's *These Are the Words: A Vocabulary of Jewish Spiritual Life.* Members of a particular denominational tradition need only ask their pastor or local bookseller to help them identify their denominational publishing house and then check that publisher's listings for books designed for beginners in the tradition.

Being actively engaged in the cultivation of our own spiritual awareness means that we are better prepared to supply some of the religious information that our children need for their own development of a spiritually reflective life. Knowing about the history, beliefs, and practices of a tradition does not dictate what our interpretations of our own spiritual experiences must be, but knowledge of how other persons of faith have understood who God is and how God acts serves as a guide for our reflections. The information we gain by researching the "why" behind beliefs and practices and the nature of the conversation about ethical issues among the generations of people who have pondered these things before us helps us frame our own understanding in a way that permits greater continuity with the past and the future.

It also prevents us and our children from turning God into a personal pet, because we are more conscious of the many ways in which people talk about God and the various implications of those interpretations for people's actions. We may choose to reject certain beliefs (women's subordination to men, the virgin birth, a literal seven-day creation) or to modify certain practices (eating or avoiding certain foods that are prohibited, wearing mandated clothing styles) because the reasons for them no longer make sense in our time. We may decide to reclaim certain beliefs (mutual submission, the spiritual nature of sexuality, the idea of a Creator) and adopt alternative practices (food and clothing choices that support companies offering fair wages and good working conditions) because they represent our contemporary interpretation of what ancient followers of our tradition were attempting to do as spiritually aware persons. Exploring these options with our children helps us appreciate how different contexts lend themselves to varied ways of living out the principles of a religious tradition.

CONCEPTS OF GOD

Preschool children may realize that their image of God is similar to how they perceive Santa Claus or a superhero, but they cannot yet comprehend the difference between their image and how that image relates to their actions. However, when school-age children and adults become more spiritually aware, we realize that sometimes what we say we think about God and how we actually relate to God are not the same. This should not be surprising, as human beings often believe one thing in theory and do contradictory things in practice. For instance, how many parents claim it is important to encourage their young children's independence and then continue to do various tasks for them in order to speed up the family's morning routine? I'm certainly guilty of this disconnection between theoretical values and practice! Relating to God engenders similar discontinuities.

Canadian Ralph Milton has a section in his book *God for Beginners* that describes "a few of the most popular ideas about God" held by persons like you and me who often live in "default" positions rather than among our ideals. Included in his list of twelve are "God the General" (who commands human activity and is always on the side of the believer against perceived enemies), "God the Computer Hack" (who set things in motion and is now too busy working on other projects to pay much attention to humanity), "God the Cop"

137

(who lies in wait to trap and punish wrongdoers), and "God the Social Worker" (who offers advice and support). Perhaps the most common operative understanding of God, in part because several religious traditions explicitly teach this image, is his "God the Parent."

> God is a very good, very caring Parent. The Parent God, traditionally referred to as Father but sometimes also as Mother, is loving and tender, and has read all the books on how to raise children to be mature and responsible adults. Parent God hurts when the kids mess up. But even so, Parent God knows that's the only way for the kids to grow. They've got to have the freedom. Totally. The Parent God respects us, and believes passionately that we can and will grow up. This Parent God gets really upset when the kids fight with each other or refuse to share things with each other.

Milton's descriptions are caricatures, yet they remind us of how much our own ordinary psychosocial experiences shape our ways of imagining the extraordinary.

The intersection of our personal experiences with our ideas about God can provide glimpses of the divine and also lead us astray. The image of God as a parent, which is commonly held by young children because of their personal experience of parents as "in charge" of their world, generally carries with it the negative experiences of parental relationships as well as the positive. Many adults operate with a combination "God as Parent/Cop" image developed out of their hyperbolized experiences of parental punishment. Others imagine "God as Parental Pushover" because they rarely experienced appropriate limit setting while they were growing up. Left unchallenged, these one-dimensional images of God limit our ability to interact with a God who is much more than our caricatures. If we continually ask ourselves and our school-age children how God is and is not like the various roles (parent, doctor, teacher, president, and so on) people have in the world, we guard against defining God too narrowly for our spiritual lives to flourish.

EXPANDING AWARENESS THROUGH INTUITION AND BODILY KNOWLEDGE

Spiritual awareness is not only a function of study and cognitive insight. Even when children and adults have developed the cognitive ability to think in complex, abstract terms, some of what we apprehend about God and the spiritual life continues to become known to us through intuitive or bodily forms of knowing. The calm assurance of God's presence with us that comes from sitting in silence is a form of spiritual awareness that may not take the shape of a particular concept or idea about God. Historically, monastic communities have been most attuned to this way of knowing God. Joan Chittister, a Benedictine sister, recounts a brief saying of the fourth-century monastics who lived in the Egyptian desert:
"A brother went to see Abba Moses in his hermitage at Scetis and begged him for a word. And the old man said: 'Go and sit in your cell, and your cell will teach you everything.'"

Although we and our children do not live in physical cells like those of the desert monastics, we, like them, need quiet places and quiet times where knowledge can come to us on its own rather than as the product of our intellectual reasoning.

Our participation in a community of faith also provides opportunities for us and our children to engage in spiritual reflection with our bodies. Bowing, kneeling, sitting, standing, swaying, clapping, processing, crossing ourselves, moving beads through our fingers, removing our shoes—all these actions teach and reteach us about God and our relationship with God each time we do them. What may begin as imitation and is sometimes rote reflex is also habituating us to certain attitudes and beliefs. Learning about these actions is one form of spiritual awareness, but our bodies also "know" and make known what we believe is important. It is often only when we realize that other people's bodies are acting differently from ours that we notice how much our bodies have learned.

We also become more conscious of our bodily knowledge when we try to pass religious practices on to our children and have to stop and think about what we do and why we do it. Despite the sometimes hidden nature of our body's knowledge, however, we shouldn't underestimate the power of bodily understanding for shaping spiritual awareness. We sometimes expect children to do as we say rather than what we do. But actions speak loudly to children, whether those actions are their own or other people's behavior. What child doesn't consciously and unconsciously try to imitate the poses and gestures of beloved adults? When some of our physical actions are linked to our spiritual practices, that knowledge is transferred in part from us to our children when they imitate us. They watch us to see whether we bow our heads or raise our hands when we pray, notice that we genuflect when we enter our place of worship, and try to kneel beside us at the altar rail. Their awareness of why we do what we do may be limited to what they surmise from the context of our actions, but their bodies take on an intuitive sense of the meaning and importance of moving in certain ways at certain times. Such bodily understandings can be hard to change if they become ingrained over several years, which is why we should pay attention to the messages we send with our bodies and alter our behavior if it doesn't match what we want our children to learn. Our actions often say more about our operative beliefs than any of our words.

One such movement is bowing one's head to pray. If we were taught to pray in this posture, or if we observed that the people around us who prayed always bowed their heads, we likely respond to an invitation to pray by immediately tucking our chin toward our chest. We associate this movement with reverence. If someone instructed us to pray with our head tilted upward and our arms stretched high, we would likely feel awkward and perhaps even irreverent in that pose, at least until our bodies became used to the new posture. Our body is aware something is different, even if our mind hasn't figured the problem out yet, and our understanding of the spiritual practice of prayer must change because of this bodily awareness if the new prayer posture is to become meaningful for us. We might say that our muscles and nerves are the source of physical reflection, just as our brain is the site of cognitive reflection. Both tell us what we understand about the spiritual life.

Combine attentiveness to these different ways of knowing with similar concern for emotional and social forms of reflection, and we

Prayer Postures

The position of our body when we pray communicates and invokes certain feelings. These associations come from our experience of these postures in our wider social interactions and from the ways in which the words we say or hear while holding such positions teach us to relate certain attitudes and experiences with a particular posture. Experiment with some of the following postures, paying attention to what your body is telling you about the meaning of each position and what your mind and heart are saying to God while praying in these ways.

Sitting a common prayer posture signifying receptivity to God that is a popular way to meditate because this position remains comfortable for extended periods of time

Kneeling a posture of penitence and humility, which many use to help them remember their need for forgiveness and signify their awareness of God's power

Standing a posture of praise and intercession, especially if accompanied by arms stretched upward

Lying prostrate a position signifying suffering and spiritual emptiness; involves lying prone on the floor with one's arms folded beneath one's head

Bowing a posture that may involve only the head or the entire torso; signifies reverence for God

Signing oneself making the sign of the cross or another religious symbol, which calls to mind in a bodily way the meaning of that symbol for the believer

have the means for nurturing an ever-deepening and broadening spiritual awareness for our children and ourselves. We can support our children as they learn to analyze and order their spiritual experiences in ways that take advantage of whatever cognitive abilities they pos-

Supporting Children as They Grow in Spiritual Awareness

sess. We can help them recognize that spiritual awareness, like spiritual experience, is multisensory and encourage them to develop spiritual beliefs and practices that are consistent with one another. We can delight in the growing store of knowledge about God that children demonstrate through the use of their minds and bodies. We may even discover that we are growing in spiritual awareness alongside them as we, too, become more attuned to what we believe and do, and why.

Chapter 7

ACTING OUT OUR SPIRITUALITY WITH CHILDREN

We often think of spirituality as relating only to our interior lives—as an internal orientation or state of being. The spiritual life certainly has such a purpose, and cultivating our contemplative nature through prayer and meditation is essential to our well-being and our relationship with God. But spirituality isn't simply in our minds and hearts. It is also in our relationships with other people and in our actions in the world. The peace, compassionate care, and moral challenges we experience in our meditative encounters with God are gifts to be shared with the world. Silence and solitude prepare us and our children to re-engage the noisiness of our communities with peaceful, compassionate, and moral actions.

It can be helpful to think of compassion and morality as forms of spiritual awareness in which our spiritual experience becomes the basis for making intentional choices about how we will live and work with others. Our external actions then become the locus of other spiritual experiences on which we meditate in our quiet times, leading to new insights and decisions about how we ought to live. This journeying inward and outward creates a rhythm for our spiritual lives that helps us balance introspection and service. When we enable our children to live and move and have their being within this balance, we

143

help them see that neither self-centeredness nor self-abnegation are worthy goals in life, despite the social pressures that might incline them toward one extreme or the other.

Two Aspects of the Spiritual Life

Imagine that we can map the spiritual life on a grid that looks a bit like a four-square court: a large box evenly divided into four smaller boxes. One side of the vertical centerline represents our spiritual journey inward; the other is the outward spiritual journey. Above the horizontal centerline represents the positive aspects of being either inwardly or outwardly focused; below that line reside the negative aspects of those foci.

A typical spiritual life moves through all four of these quadrants as a matter of course.

The positive Journey Inward represents the contemplative practices in a person's life—the times we and our children spend pushing

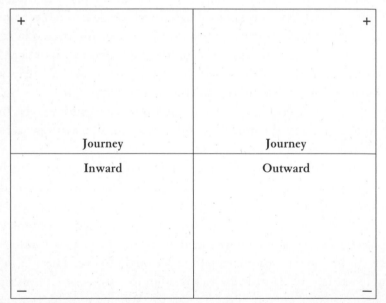

The Dynamics of Spirituality

aside the noisiness of the world so we can attend to God's presence and God's voice. When we dwell in this space, we are in listening mode, inviting the silence or the words and images of others to "speak" a word from God. Here the stories, music, artwork, and unseen presence of God nourish our spirit and draw us closer to the essence of our being as persons created in the image of God. Here our experiences as part of a religious community infuse our identity. Within us, God tills the ground so that enduring values and commitments can take root and grow in spiritual soil that is fertile and deep. The Journey Inward is where we practice living in relationship with God.

The danger of journeying inward is that we can become so enamored of the peacefulness and comfort we hope to find there that we retreat into full-time self-fulfillment. We start to meditate because it feels good; we pray because we want God to fulfill our personal desires; we focus so much attention on getting our lives in order and becoming personal success stories that we no longer care about what is happening in other people's lives, except as those events impinge on our own happiness. Sociologists called the 1980s the "Me" decade because so many people felt justified in putting their own self-fulfillment first that the concept of social responsibility held little sway in discussions about business ethics and community services. The twenty-first century has brought a reawakening of interest in community building, although the terrorist acts in the United States on September 11, 2001 and the resultant world unrest continue to encourage many people to reside in the negative (escapism) quadrant of the inward journey.

The positive aspects of the Journey Outward emanate from our engagement in relationships of hospitality and justice in our neighborhoods and the world. When we and our children serve others, we experience the pleasure of human connections, the satisfaction of contributing to something larger than ourselves, and the opportunity to learn new and intriguing ideas from a variety of people. We discover unexpected things about ourselves as well: abilities we didn't realize we have, assumptions that may not serve us well, and allegiances that can reshape the world as a better place for everyone. We realize that

Acting Out Our Spirituality with Children

we are not alone and that our neighbors need our particular gifts just as we need what they have to offer. The Journey Outward is where we practice living in community with God's people.

Most of us already know, however, that living in unmitigated service to others quickly leads to exhaustion and burnout. Women, in particular, have been encouraged to set aside their own needs and desires in order to nurture and support the needs and ambitions of men and children. Workers of both sexes feel the pressure to serve the goals of their workplaces to the exclusion of sufficient time for reflection, self-care, and family life. Requests for financial contributions and volunteerism make their way to us by phone, mail, and e-mail on a near-daily basis. We already devote much of our time to providing for the needs of our children, who are themselves responding to numerous solicitations for fundraising and for participating in service projects and organizations. We may feel guilty daily about the worthwhile things we say no to, even as we struggle to keep up with the ones to which we've assented. Unrelenting service can make us slaves to the expectations of others or our own inflated sense of importance and indispensability.

Balance in our spiritual life comes from regular movement through the quadrants of the Journey Inward–Journey Outward grid in a figure-8 motion. Whenever we sense that we are moving below the horizontal centerline from the positive aspects of one half of the spiritual journey into the negative aspects, we correct for that side's dangers by shifting into the diagonally opposite positive quadrant. Hence, when our inward reflection becomes tinged with the desire to dwell in passive acquiescence toward social concerns that don't directly affect us, we remind ourselves through an intentional movement into service that no one remains unaffected when injustice goes unchallenged. When we feel overwhelmed by the world's neediness or recognize that we are developing an "us-them" mentality that inflates our importance and denigrates those we serve, we intentionally seek to spend more time in silence and reflection with the source of all power and creativity.

We might believe that we can dwell only in the upper half of the grid, and if we were capable of perfection, we would be right. One goal of a robust spiritual life, however, is to be attentive to the un-

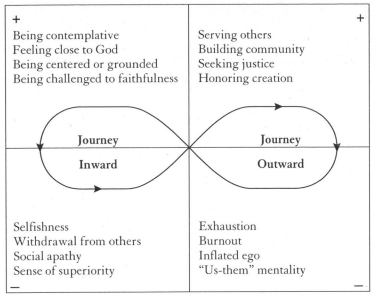

+	+
Being contemplative	Serving others
Feeling close to God	Building community
Being centered or grounded	Seeking justice
Being challenged to faithfulness	Honoring creation
Journey Inward	**Journey Outward**
Selfishness	Exhaustion
Withdrawal from others	Burnout
Social apathy	Inflated ego
Sense of superiority	"Us-them" mentality
−	−

A Map of Our Spiritual Journey

avoidable movements below that line so that we can redirect our energies and attention toward one positive aspect or the other. The loops in our figure-8 should become higher and fuller in the upper domains and shallower in the lower region as we learn to say yes to the appropriate mix of inward and outward activities and no to those actions and inclinations that pull us away from love of God and neighbor.

Helping Children Find a Spiritual Balance

Children, like adults, will gravitate toward the missing spiritual element in their lives if the adults around them help provide opportunities for inward reflection or outward service. The mother of a first grader whose church school class emphasized silence and meditation as part of its regular practice told me that her son decided to "share silence" with his public school classmates during show-and-tell. "He works on silence for himself—it's hard for him," she reported, and yet she recognized that his efforts were because he felt a need for silent reflection time and thought his friends would appreciate such time as

Acting Out Our Spirituality with Children

well. In many ways, this child is inviting himself and his friends to take a time out, without the connotations of punishment associated with that practice. Another mother recalled her embarrassment as well as her pride when her seven-year-old daughter became really excited about collecting shoes for a church drive, with the theme of following Jesus' commandment to care for the poor. "[She] wanted to make announcements at school. She asked out-of-town relatives for shoes when we went there for Thanksgiving." Her daughter was exhibiting a zeal for the outward spiritual journey rooted in her inward reflection on a religious teaching and the sense that anything less than an all-out effort would be apathetic.

Not all children, however, are as attuned to their own spiritual needs as these younger elementary students. Every parent has contended with the overstimulated child who throws a tantrum because he or she doesn't recognize the internal signal that it's time to withdraw into a quieter place and reconnect with the center of being. Selfishness and disregard for the needs and feelings of others is also a common part of childhood, learned as much from the callousness of adults as from the human inclination toward self-preservation. Adults have a responsibility to help children notice the ways in which they are operating below the horizontal centerline of the spirituality grid and brainstorm together about ways of correcting course.

As I observed a group of sixth graders, I heard one child tell a family story about going to buy contact lenses and seeing homeless men holding up signs by the highway exit requesting work or other help. The girl reported that her mother locked the doors of the car and kept driving. The rest of the children responded that they thought holding up signs about being homeless was "stupid" and "a waste of rich people's time." The mother's actions, coupled with other messages the children had heard about persons who are homeless, reinforced the us-them mentality these children were developing in their outward spiritual journey. A parental act most likely intended to ensure safety provoked a different interpretive use among these preteens—a use that indicated a need to move into a spiritually reflective mode. An astute adult listening to their comments could invite such reflection.

Journeying Outward with Children

In Chapter Five, I suggested several ways in which adults and children can engage in the contemplative aspects of the spiritual life. In this chapter, we focus our attention on how we can nurture children in a life of compassionate service. Conventional wisdom suggests that children are both naturally self-centered (hence their difficulty sharing their possessions) and naturally affectionate and caring. The bickering that goes on between siblings and playmates more often draws our attention to the former behavior, with genuinely compassionate actions stemming from the latter surprising us because we seldom prepare ourselves to handle childhood empathy. But a parent told me the story of her children's reactions to the news that they would be hosting, in their home, a sixteen-year-old girl from another state who needed a place to stay before a medical procedure. Her eight-year-old daughter asked why the girl's family wasn't going to be with her, and the mother explained that they couldn't come. Her four-and-a-half-year-old son replied, "It doesn't matter. If she needs a house, Jesus says we're supposed to give her one."

The older child's question seemed normal to this mother, but the younger child's declaration took her by delighted surprise. Here was "proof" that her preschool son was making the connection between the values of his faith tradition and his family's activities of service to those in need. Here, too, is one clue as to how families can encourage the life of service.

Children imitate the actions of those around them. As Robert Coles has noted, "Our children add up, imitate, file away what they've observed and so very often later fall in line with the particular moral counsel we wittingly or quite unself-consciously have offered them." They tend to interpret the activities of their household as norms against which other people's activities are measured. Even when they argue with parents that "so-and-so's family doesn't do it that way" or "everybody else's parents let them," their intent is more to test the elasticity of the family's way of being than to topple the normative infrastructure altogether. So if their family regularly goes out of its way to help persons in need, they will most likely see such activity as constitutive of their identity and participate in similar acts of service themselves. Their inner reflection on and acceptance of the family's values will generate a desire to live out those values in concrete ways.

Children will also ponder information they have gotten from trusted adults and then shape their actions to match their conclusions about that information. They may enact what they have learned because they desire (consciously or unconsciously) to please the adults who taught them, but primarily they embody their beliefs because that is how young children's minds work. Their concrete thinking leads them to follow ideas through to their logical conclusion, often with a degree of literalness that surprises adults. Six months after the September 11 terrorist attacks, a church school teacher asked a group of first through third graders, "Do you think Osama bin Laden follows the Golden Rule?" The children quickly answered, "No way!" But then one girl said, "But I still want to pray for him," and a boy added, "Every night I pray for peace and that the people over there will win." Past lessons about praying for others, a bedtime ritual, and the day's discussion of Jesus' commandment to "do unto others as you would have them do unto you" was leading these children to concrete actions: daily prayers for bin Laden and for a peaceful outcome of the military activity in the region.

PRAYER AS A FORM OF SERVICE

We might not think of prayer as a way of serving others, and yet intercessory prayer is one means by which we act on behalf of those in trouble in hope that their situation will be transformed. Some monastic communities devote themselves to prayer for the world as their primary work. In Indianapolis, where I live, the members of the Roman Catholic Carmelite community "pray the news" daily and encourage people to call or e-mail their prayer requests so that the sisters can include the personal concerns of the city's residents in their intercessions. They explain why on their Web site, www.praythe news.com.

We look. . . . and all too often, it seems, there is no one to help. No one, it seems, to free the oppressed, uphold the fallen, or shelter the homeless. We may view these events through a television screen, the front page of a newspaper—or even the eyes of someone who has seen. However they come to us, these painful reminders of the incompleteness of the world are everywhere. It is in this context, then, that we pray the news. By continuously making ourselves aware of the present moment of the universe, we awaken ourselves to our presence to God—and in our own way, participate in the healing, loving and creative energy this process can spark.

Like the sisters and their many counterparts in various religious traditions, we can engage in "a life of active prayer for the world" as part of our outward spiritual journey with our children. It may be that our children even take the lead in this endeavor with their desires to pray for those others label as enemies as well as those close to heart and home.

Compassionate Actions

In addition to praying for those in need, acting out one's inward spiritual convictions requires exhibiting compassion for others. The Prophet Muhammad, father of Islam, asked his followers, "What actions are most excellent?" He answered his own question, "To gladden the heart of human beings, to feed the hungry, to help the afflicted, to lighten the sorrow of the sorrowful, and to remove the sufferings of the injured." One of the Five Pillars of Islam is *Zakat,* or almsgiving. To show compassion for the poor, Muslim families are expected to give 2.5 percent of their income to charity. The Quran also encourages Muslims to engage in voluntary service that aids those less fortunate than themselves. Compassionate acts are not optional in Islamic spirituality; they are an essential aspect of a holistic spiritual journey.

Judaism has similar expectations of its adherents. During the festival of Purim, families traditionally practice *matanot l'evyonim,* the provision of basic goods (clothes, food, and money for shelter) for the poor in their community. The practice of *bikur cholim,* in which families visit sick neighbors to offer comfort and support, is also emphasized by Jewish tradition. The eighth-century Jewish prophet Micah, in the scriptural book of the same name, posed his followers a question similar to that of Mohammad: "What does the Lord require of you but to do justice, and to love kindness, and to walk humbly with your God?" (Micah 6:8).

This combination query and declaration is embraced by Christians as well as part of their shared biblical heritage with Judaism. Another shared conviction derives from the Jewish and Christian scriptural claims that the second greatest commandment from God is the love of neighbor (the first being love of God). In the writings of the Apostle Paul, several of the Ten Commandments from the Hebrew Bible ("You shall not commit adultery," "You shall not murder," "You shall not steal," "You shall not covet . . .") are summed up in this phrase, "Love your neighbor as yourself" (Romans 13:9). Most of us refrain from blatantly violating the prohibitions that underlie this "Golden Rule." We actively teach our children not to covet one another's belongings when we encourage them to share. We exact consequences when they hit or push another child in anger so that they will learn to refrain from violence. We encourage our teens to develop honest dating relationships that put fidelity to a current boyfriend or girlfriend high on their list of priorities. We refuse to condone stealing (we march a child back to the convenience store to return the pack of gum taken in a moment of temptation). We may set a variety of prohibitions around teasing, belittling, or bullying others so that our children will learn to treat others as they wish to be treated. All of these commonplace activities of parenting encourage our children to live as compassionate persons in the world. They help children put into action the internal values they are developing as part of their reflections on the meaning of life.

But engaging in the outward spiritual journey also pushes us to show compassion for those whose circumstances in life—homelessness, poverty, incarceration, illness, lack of education—could lead to their death or to continued deprivation of material goods and services necessary for their well-being. Although some of these persons may reside within our circle of family and friends, many more are strangers. Caring for them moves us out of our comfort zone and may even illuminate tensions among our internal ideals and our lifestyle.

Children are especially sensitized to the discrepancies between words and actions because they have not yet learned to weigh the pros and cons of a particular action in terms of complex relationships. If they see someone on the street wearing ragged clothing and asking for financial help, they may presume that the obvious solution is to give the person money to buy food and better clothes. Going shopping is how families take care of their needs, so they move logically to supply what appears to be the missing link in this other person's comparable situation: money with which to shop. They do not stop to consider, as their adult companions are likely to do, whether mental illness, alcoholism, drug abuse, or some other problem might be a factor that renders the question of whether to give money more complicated. They may not know, unless they are at least school-age and have discussed such things with parents and teachers, that there are systemic reasons for homelessness that a single gift of money cannot resolve. Our own spiritual reflection on our responsibility to love our neighbors as ourselves must become our guide to discussing this responsibility with our children, even as our children's seemingly naïve questions may be what prompt us to reflect on this issue at all.

Acting for the Sake of Justice

The spiritual life of service sometimes leads children and adults to act in ways that will bring justice in an unjust situation. Jewish author and social worker Janice Cohn tells the true story of how the people of Billings, Montana, responded to hate crimes in their town. Her book *The Christmas Menorahs: How a Town Fought Hate* focuses especially on the actions of two elementary classmates and their families when one of them has his home vandalized because he's Jewish. The children, Isaac Schnitzer and Teresa Hanley, each decide to stand up for what they believe in, in part because the adults around them encourage reflective action. Isaac, at the invitation of his teacher,

Activities for Encouraging Compassion

Jolene Roehlkepartain has collected over three hundred ideas for fostering compassion in her book *Teaching Kids to Care & Share.* Try out some of her ideas (described next), or let them spark new possibilities for you and your family.

- Organize a baby-blanket drive. Contact a local hospital, low-income child-care center, police station, or child protection agency to see who would benefit and be willing to work with you.
- Talk about different situations in which someone seems left out. Encourage your child to notice these people and to reach out to children (and to adults only when accompanied by an adult they know) to help people feel included. For example, a child can sit by a new child at school to help him feel included or team up with a parent to visit a neighbor who lives alone, just to say hello.
- Create "Care Bags" for children in hospitals or at home with long-term illnesses. Brainstorm with your child about things

decides to tell his predominantly Christian classmates the story of Hanukkah so they will understand why Jewish families place menorahs in their windows as part of their holiday celebration. Teresa convinces her family to draw a picture of a menorah and put it up on their living-room window as a sign of solidarity with Isaac and his family. Adults and children throughout Billings band together to paper thousands of non-Jewish homes and businesses with printed menorahs, thus confounding the attempt by a group of skinheads to intimidate Jewish families.

Isaac and Teresa are examples of children who exhibit moral character. Robert Coles says that "character is ultimately who we are that would be good for someone who is sick. Items might include crayons, markers, tablets of plain paper, coloring books, puzzle books, stickers, books, trading cards, and so on. Use one-gallon zipper bags to hold the items.

- Clean a playground. Pick up trash. Create a lost-and-found area for items that have been left. Sweep all the sand or pea gravel off the slides and swings. Remove sticks, leaves, grass, and other debris from sandboxes.

- Give your child a UNICEF collection box on Halloween to collect coins from people in addition to treats. This encourages your child to think of others, in addition to themselves, on this holiday. Boxes can be obtained by contacting UNICEF at 1–800-FOR-KIDS.

- Arrange for your older children to receive training in CPR and the Heimlich maneuver. Children who know these emergency procedures have used them on occasion and literally saved lives. Practice these techniques and talk about why learning them is important. Many local YMCAs and Jewish Community Centers offer babysitting or first-aid courses for children ten and older that include basic rescue training.

expressed in action, in how we live, in what we do . . ." It is our true internal commitments converted into specific interactions with the world around us. It is, to quote the fourth-century Christian, Saint Augustine, to "sing a new song not with our lips but with our lives." Children's keen interest in fairness presents an opportunity for adults to encourage them to brainstorm ways they can create a more just local and world community and then to support them in implementing those ideas. Sometimes that means talking frankly with our children about how we attempt to balance our desire for a safe and comfortable lifestyle with the risks and disruptions of such a lifestyle that come from engaging in social action.

Janice Cohn tells another story of a child who saw a news program on homelessness and decided he wanted to take the blanket from his bed and give it to a homeless person that very evening. His parents, after getting over their initial shock at his declaration, discussed the risks involved and decided to accompany him downtown to do as he wanted. They then supported the eleven-year-old as he initiated a citywide blanket campaign to help keep homeless persons warm in Philadelphia—a campaign that eventually led to the establishment of a shelter, thrift store, and job training center as well. The parents' initial misgivings are easy for us to understand, but their method of encouraging their son's outward spiritual journey through thoughtful engagement in service can be a model for our own family's reflective action.

Above my desk hangs a drawing from my daughter. Sitting in congregational worship one October Sunday morning, she sketched a large flower, shaded its petals and leaves carefully with her pencil, and then wrote above it, "Stand up for what you believe in even if you're standing alone." She inscribed it to me from her and then passed it across her younger brother to where I sat in the pew. I don't know why she combined the flower with those particular words, or why she gave the drawing to me. At the time I neglected to ask her about it. But that sheet of paper reminds me of how children are wrestling with the relationship between beliefs and actions, even when there is no obvious trigger for those reflections. Neither the church school lesson nor the sermon for that day explicitly addressed the issues of perseverance or justice, but my daughter had such concerns on her mind. Had I asked her to tell me more about her drawing, we might have wondered together about specific ways we might stand up for something important. Fortunately, other opportunities for brainstorming and action have presented themselves since that time, for children care deeply about the world and will offer adults many chances to care with them before coming to the conclusion that justice isn't really important in an adult world.

Principles of Social Justice

Kathleen and James McGinnis are Christians and staff members of the Institute for Peace and Justice in St. Louis, Missouri. Here are the six basic principles for involving children in social justice activities that they have followed as parents and organizers, reproduced from their book, *Parenting for Peace and Justice.*

1. We regularly invite children to join us in social action. (This invitation, however, includes the freedom for children to decline and a commitment to make decisions about involvement as a family.)
2. Broad exposure to advocates, victims, situations, is crucial. (Children need to meet others involved in the struggle for social justice and have age-appropriate experiences with those who are victims of injustice.)
3. We try to invite the children to actions that are within their capabilities. (For younger children, this generally means actions related to family life or prior experiences; for all children, there needs to be a specific role they can take.)
4. We try to integrate fun whenever possible. (Fun can be generated by banding together with other families, planning a celebration in connection with one's work, or adding artistic flourishes to signs and letters.)
5. Social action involvement means "doing with" rather than "doing for." (This means helping children recognize the gifts that those they assist share with them in turn.)
6. Social action involves the works of justice as well as the works of mercy. (Economic and political advocacy and even civil disobedience may be necessary before justice is realized.)

Being "Different"

Living a life of spiritual service can fit neatly into a comfortable lifestyle that remains mostly hidden away from people outside our households. We may make choices like reducing our use of disposable products, reusing plastic containers, and recycling soda cans and glass jars because we want to enact a commitment to sharing the world's resources more fairly with people in distant lands, and no one is likely to ask us to justify our decision because "reduce, reuse, recycle" is one of the socially acceptable mantras of our time. People put their recycling bin out by the curb weekly for a variety of reasons; only some of them would call their actions spiritually inspired. The same is true for a certain level of benevolence. Payroll deductions for United Way, change tossed in the Salvation Army pot during December, and the donation of unwanted household items to Goodwill rarely attract attention because such actions are commonplace. Children who know about or participate in these activities learn a level of compassion consistent with the customary practices of their social peers.

The ongoing challenge of loving our neighbors as ourselves, however, can generate actions that stand out from the social norm. It is rare for a family to respond to a news story about homelessness by taking their own blankets and heading downtown in search of someone in greater need of a covering than themselves. Other people may not understand why we might choose to do such a thing. Trevor, the boy in Cohn's account, endured ridicule at school for his actions. "They called him a goody-goody or 'blanket boy,'" his father told Cohn. Even with the contemporary emphasis on community service projects in schools, significant investment in helping others can result in a child's being teased for acting differently from his or her peers. The developmental task of learning how to balance conformity and differentiation in order to participate in one's social networks continually complicates our older children's decisions about when and how to serve others.

It may also create new tensions for us as adults because we want our children to be well received by their peers. Trevor's parents admitted that they weren't as supportive of their son amidst the teasing as they could have been because they, too, thought at first that Trevor was going too far. His mother told Cohn, "I thought Trevor was crazy—insane—to want to do this. Now I work with him in the thrift store, which is in a terrible, drug-infested area. There are shootings and violence, and my friends think I'm crazy to be there. But I like it. The people we deal with are so real."

Whether the idea for an unusual level of family service generates from a child's enthusiasm or parental commitments, we have to contend with what our friends and neighbors think. The degree to which we can handle being labeled "crazy" has an effect on our ability to participate in the outward spiritual journey as fully as our inward reflections might prompt us and our children to do.

Cultivating "Crazy" Friends

One of the ways to increase our degree of comfort with "crazy" levels of service is to invite friends and family members to join us in shared expressions of compassion and justice. Knowing that another family "like ours" is spending their Thanksgiving serving dinner at a shelter or forgoing a DVD player in order to make a sizeable contribution to a hunger relief organization helps children see these actions as normative in some households, even if they are not commonplace. My children sometimes complain about our lack of cable television, high-speed Internet access, and a cell phone. Yet when we talk about the various reasons we choose not to have these things, the one that makes the most sense to them is our explanation that we give a set percentage of our family income away each year for the benefit of others, thus voluntarily limiting our spending power. (They are less enamored of the explanations related to parental censorship of media exposure and a quest for a simpler lifestyle, thinking us hopelessly out of touch with contemporary reality!)

My children accept the benevolence explanation more easily, in part, because they know other families who do the same thing. Their friends' families may choose to eat out less in order to have money to share or to purchase cable rather than spend a larger amount of money on video rentals. They may set a spending limit on holiday gifts and donate a matching amount to charity. The choices families make to free themselves for giving need not be identical for children to see the relationship between voluntarily forgoing something others do or have in order to care for someone deprived of basic necessities.

The companionship of friends also serves as an antidote to the fears that acts of justice seeking may evoke. To "stand up for what you believe in even if you're standing alone" is both a laudable goal and a state in which none of us would prefer to find ourselves. Having two or three friends by our side emboldens us. It insulates us somewhat from accusations of irrationality and strangeness because we know others share our perspective and commitment. It provides a check on the inevitable defensiveness that challenges to our stand elicit. It may even be the means by which our children, like Isaac, Teresa, and Trevor, accomplish something amazing in their community.

VALUING CHILDREN'S CONTRIBUTIONS

In the fall of 1994, a friend of our family and instructor at Harvard Divinity School decided to run for lieutenant governor of Massachusetts. Bob had never run for political office before, but he believed that the commonwealth needed someone in statewide office who would advocate for policies and practices conducive to creating a true place of "common wealth." I and a bunch of other idealistic doctoral students became his initial campaign committee. Already overly busy trying to balance parenting, dissertation writing, and teaching responsibilities, I carted my seven- and three-year-olds with me to strategy meetings, envelope-stuffing parties, and stints on street corners holding up signs. My three-year-old daughter didn't really understand the significance of what we were doing, but my seven-year-old son was forming opinions and making decisions about his own involvement in the campaign alongside everyone else.

One requirement for getting on the ballot in Massachusetts is amassing ten thousand signatures from registered voters in one's political party. My son decided that he wanted to help collect signatures.

He would stand with his father outside shopping malls and town halls asking people to sign Bob's ballot petition. When asked why he thought Bob ought to be elected, he told people, "Well, I don't like all the violence everywhere. And I think that people should be able to go to the doctor when they're sick, even if they don't have a lot of money. Someone might have a bad accident or something. You never know." Having listened to Bob and the various adults in his campaign talk about the issues, our son believed that Bob, if elected, would help make new laws that would bring an end to violence and provide health care for everyone.

Perhaps he would have come to these same conclusions just by listening to his father and me talk about our work on the campaign. But being in the midst of the action gave him the sense that even young children can make a difference through their thoughtful service. Each signature he collected put the campaign closer to the ten thousand required. His enthusiasm inspired the other workers when Bob was running behind in the polls, and the respect of the adults in the campaign for his ideas and interpretations instilled in him an abiding desire to help others, even when Bob lost the general election. The presence of our son and daughter and the children of other volunteers wasn't simply tolerated by Bob and the other adults active in his campaign. Their contributions, small and large, were valued as part of the "common wealth" of resources necessary for transforming society. We reinforce children's desire to journey outward when we find them places to serve among adults congenial to their presence.

NURTURING A LIFETIME OF SERVICE

Whether we choose to work as a family in a political campaign, volunteer time serving meals to the homeless, cultivate a garden to share with homebound neighbors, visit residents of a nursing home once a month, help organize educational events to combat racism, or set aside a significant portion of family income for charitable causes, we are acting out our spirituality with our children in ways they will remember all their lives. Jan Johnson, author of *Growing Compassionate Kids,*

Acting Out Our Spirituality with Children

tells of interviewing an acquaintance who was planning to serve in the Peace Corps between college and taking her first job. The young woman, Heidi, recalled, "My parents talked about starving people in Ethiopia all the time. We groaned about that stuff—that frustrated my parents. It was important that they tried. It had an impact later in life, even if I wasn't paying attention too much at the time." Heidi's family not only talked about the relationship between hungry strangers half a world away but they made purchasing choices based on their commitment to encourage a more just global economy and regularly helped homeless people in their own town get a hot meal. They shaped Heidi and her siblings in an ethic of caring that included reflection on the needs of the world and action to meet those needs.

A full spiritual life for us and our children combines these elements of reflection and action in a never-ending movement of journeying inward toward God and outward toward neighbors who are both friends and strangers. Not every child need choose to enter the Peace Corps as a result of what he or she experiences at home. But children can grow up seeing the world as a place where their actions make a difference because of their commitment to be consistent in their inward and outward selves, especially if they have loving adults beside them who see themselves the same way.

Conclusion

FINDING A FAITH COMMUNITY TO CALL YOUR OWN

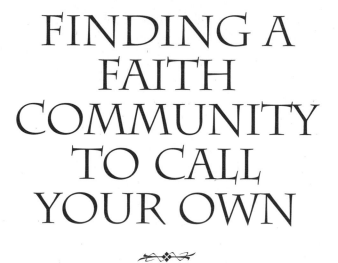

The process of nurturing and sustaining children in a life of faith is exhilarating because it calls forth in us our own spiritual longings and commitments and provides ways to live well with them. We get to ponder alongside our children the mystery of God's presence and activity in the world. We revel with them in times of being silent and resting in God's love. We practice speaking a new language together and telling stories that give meaning to our lives. We get to ask ourselves what items we will include in our household as signs of the religious culture that shapes our spiritual journey. We act out our deepest commitments through shared service in a larger world that needs our love and care. Our lives no longer revolve mostly around to-do lists on which we check off tasks in order to get through each day responsibly. We instead reclaim the lost dimension of divine love that can nurture and sustain our own spiritual lives, even as we nurture and sustain those of our children.

Don't Go It Alone

This process can be exhausting, however, if undertaken alone by a single parent or one set of parents. Like Anne Lamott and her son, Sam, we need a community of faithful people to study, work, pray, and worship alongside us and our children so that we need not shoulder the responsibility in isolation from the resources others can provide. In many ways, we are like contemporary homeschoolers who assume primary responsibility for their children's education and yet regularly come together with other homeschooling families to create opportunities for shared learning, participation in sports or other large-group experiences, supplemental resources, and the challenge of building relationships and discussing ideas with those outside one's immediate circle.

Parents are the principal guides in children's spiritual formation, yet children need a religious community within which to experience God as something other than their own friend or possession. They need the benefit of others' discoveries about divine love and others' testimonies to the challenges of faithful living. They need to rub up against different ideas about God and experience the affirmation of shared understanding. They need opportunities to be shaped by communal rituals and practices that extend beyond the narrow confines of their immediate family so that they realize their kinship with other spiritual people. They need to recognize that their religious language belongs to many others and that they can speak this language outside the home as well as within it. Affiliation with a religious community provides children with the kind of extensive and diverse support that no one or two individuals can provide, given the limitations of human time, energy, and experience. As Lamott says, a community of faith provides children with a "brighter light than the glimmer of their own candle" or even the glow from a few family candles held close beside one another.

CRITERIA FOR THE SEARCH

How, then, do families find a faith community that will nurture and sustain them in their spiritual journey? The temptation may be to simply locate the nearest congregation that has an active children's program and seems populated with nice people who look, sound, and act a lot like ourselves. Such a congregation may indeed be a place in which we can find people of spiritual depth and support for journeying inward and outward, but these two criteria may be misleading. Children's programming may focus more on teaching a set of specific points or providing religiously tinted entertainment than nurturing a vibrant relationship with God and practicing the faith together. Associating with people who only look like us may deprive us of the chance to learn from those whose experiences and ideas are significantly different from our own. Children today are particularly savvy at spotting the deficiencies of a program that doesn't really take them and their questions seriously. They may enjoy religious entertainment, but they are unlikely to let something they recognize as cultural "fluff" have much say in how they shape their core commitments and lifelong vocation. Contemporary children are also more aware than we adults were at a young age of the multicultural nature of the world. When they encounter persons of other faith traditions or other religious communities at school or in their neighborhood, they need some experience negotiating among a variety of perspectives on God's activity in the world. A diverse faith community may provide greater opportunity for acquiring such experience than a homogenous one.

Openness to the Topic of Children's Spirituality

Rather than a preference for convenience, program size, or homogeneity, our search for a faith community in which to raise a family needs to emphasize other markers of spiritual engagement and attentiveness. One such marker is openness on the part of congregational leaders to ask questions about the community's understanding of the spiritual life and children's participation in it. A pastor or religious leader who is uncomfortable talking about spirituality or cannot identify specific ways in which a congregation is seeking to form people in faith is unlikely to provide support for parents in their attempts to create a religious culture and adopt a religious language richly nuanced enough to resist collapse into competing cultures and languages. Spirituality may be something intangible in its more mystical manifestations, but the shaping of the spiritual life is an intentional activity that requires ongoing thoughtfulness on the part of faith communities. A religious leader who has not spent time pondering the ways in which a particular congregation facilitates spiritual experiences and encourages spiritual awareness cannot be a full collaborator in parenting spiritually enlivened children.

Welcome of Children Fully into the Community's Life

Another mark of a congregation's ability to nurture children's spirituality is its commitment to welcome children into all aspects of community life as participants, according to their abilities. Given the propensity in North American culture for children's activities to be segregated from adult pastimes, many religious communities operate with a separatist mentality that mimics wider practices. Adults participate in "congregational worship" and serve on committees that conduct the business of the community, and children are relegated to classrooms and children's worship. The generations may come together only during times set aside for socialization, and, even then, adults and children may congregate around separate tables or in separate parts of the room. This may seem like a comfortable way to meet everyone's needs for peer interaction, yet it also reinforces implicit rules about who belongs where and whose norms shape particular aspects of community life. A congregation that is committed to children's full belonging in the community of faith works conscientiously to create intergenerational worship and learning opportunities, reinforcing the idea that adults and children sojourn together in the spiritual life.

It takes ongoing effort for a faith community to be inclusive of all ages. When we are participating in a worship service, we can look

Inquiring About a Congregation's Openness

When my family moves to a new community, I begin our search for a faith community with a series of phone calls to congregations in our tradition that meet within a reasonable distance from our home. I have a set of questions jotted down on a notepad that guide my conversation with whichever congregational leader is available to talk with me. (I learned this strategy from experts in the field of child-care referral.) Sometimes I chat informally with the office staff person as well, especially if I have to leave a message and wait for a return call. Here are the questions likely to be on my list:

- How would you describe your congregation?
- What are the most important aspects of your congregation's life together?
- How does your congregation nurture children's spirituality?
- Who are the teachers in your children's programs?
- What resources do you have to support my spiritual formation as an adult and parent?
- How do children participate in worship?
- What kinds of commitments do you expect from families who are members of your congregation?

If the person with whom I'm talking responds to my questions primarily with a recitation of programs for children and the schedule of worship services, I follow up by asking for more detailed descriptions of what happens in those events. My goal is to obtain enough information about the values and practices of a congregation to judge whether it is a community of faith that will nurture and challenge my family to be more faithful in our spiritual lives.

for several signs indicating that a congregation is making such an effort: (1) worship leaders should be incorporating illustrations from children's experiences in their sermons; (2) corporate prayers and responsive readings should include references to children's lives, and (3) hymns and songs should attend to the multiple comprehension levels represented by an intergenerational congregation. Children who are able should be among those who read the scripture texts aloud each week. Children's choirs should participate in the service of worship as leaders in ways similar to the role filled by the adult choir if the two groups of singers are constituted separately. Adult members should appear comfortable with the inevitable sounds and small movements of the young children among them. Children should be among those greeting visitors, distributing service bulletins, collecting offerings, making announcements, serving communion elements, or engaging in any other activity that involves adult volunteers and doesn't require capabilities beyond a child's developmental reach. A teen may be running the sound board; children may bring the communion elements to the table, and a third grader may raise her hand to share a prayer concern when the congregation is invited to offer prayers of the people. Not all these things happen in every worship service, and some may not be appropriate within the theological perspective of certain traditions. But if congregational worship seems to function as an adult experience to which children are admitted only if they act like little adults, a faith community is not truly welcoming their younger members.

This is not to say that congregational worship should be a child-oriented experience to which adults are invited as chaperones. Some "family services" are so geared to the perceived needs of children (for example, using Bible storybooks in place of the scripture texts and children's songs or simple praise choruses exclusively) that the adults present receive no sustenance for their own spiritual journey. A good intergenerational worship service, in which every participant hears the call to faithfulness proclaimed in language and actions he or she can comprehend several times during the gathering, welcomes children along with persons of all other ages. It offers children access to a richly textured worship experience, through which are woven great

Ways to Know if Children Are Welcome in Worship

Janet Eibner and Susan Walker have developed a list of questions to help parents and other adults determine whether children are welcomed into congregational worship spaces as part of the greeting and worship routines practiced by a faith community. They note that greetings, which function as "official" welcoming rituals, may give children their first impressions of worship. When you visit a congregation, keep these adaptations of their seven questions in mind:

1. How are your children welcomed into the building?
2. In general, how are you and your children helped to feel comfortable?
3. Is the welcome child-centered for children and adult-centered for adults?
4. Do greeters seek the comfort of your children as they try to make sense of an unfamiliar setting and unfamiliar activities?
5. Is the service easy for children to follow?
6. Are there printed materials for children (activity sheets, a child-friendly service bulletin, coloring materials)?
7. How do children know when to do what during the service and after?

hymns and simple songs, ancient words and contemporary experiences, and opportunities for children to see and be seen by adults as worshippers.

Another sign that children are welcomed by a faith community is the commitment by a congregation to improving the lives of children in their neighborhood, whether those children are members of the congregation or not. A Presbyterian church I visited in New Mexico demonstrated this commitment by developing an after-school program for elementary children in its mixed-income neighborhood. A congregation in Boston combines a summer lunch program with an arts enrichment camp designed to bridge the vacation gap of the federal school lunch subsidy program and encourage self-esteem and artistic expression among lower-income children and youth. A small Lutheran church in Oklahoma runs a large tutoring program for children at a nearby school, even though there are very few children among the congregation's members. This same church built a playground for the neighborhood on its property as a service to the community. Faith communities may serve as designated "safe houses" for children who feel threatened as they walk to and from school. They may sponsor music education programs or create child-care centers for working parents. Sometimes such programs function more as auxiliary activities or rental arrangements than congregational ministries and therefore may not represent a true welcome of children into the life of the faith community. Parents need to ask program directors about their relationship to the rest of the congregation's activities to get an accurate picture of what services for children mean.

Commitment to Nurturing Relationships

A third mark of a faith community's interest in supporting children's spiritual formation is its commitment to programming structures that give preference to long-term relationships between adults and children over convenience and minimal engagement on the part of adult leaders. Congregations are largely volunteer organizations. In order to attract enough people to fill all the perceived leadership roles necessary for the organization to function, some congregations promise volunteers short tenures and minimal expectations as to the preparation required of them in exchange for their agreement to serve. When this orientation is used to recruit teachers for children's religious education classes and other gatherings, relationship building takes a back seat to simply getting through an event with enough hands to do the assigned task. Children have little opportunity to observe adults living the faith week after week, nor do they develop the kind of trust necessary to question and explore their spirituality and faith tradition deeply with a more experienced Christian companion. And adults miss the chance to get to know children well enough to hear beyond their immediate words to the issues and concerns that populate their worlds and foster spiritual experiences and reflection. Faith communities that are committed to nurturing relationships of spiritual exploration between adults and children ask adults to make significant commitments of time and energy to the work of accompanying children in their spiritual journey. Parents should expect the same low turnover rates among religious program leaders that they desire in a high-quality school or preschool setting.

There are many creative ways that religious communities invite adults to dwell with children over time, despite the undisputed busyness of most adult lives. Some congregations recruit pairs of adults who alternate teaching a religious education class for a school or calendar year. This allows some flexibility in scheduling around inevitable absences due to family and job responsibilities and divides the preparation labor in half for each teacher. A congregation I served, in which children's church school overlapped with congregational worship, devised an approach in which three teachers divided the work of a two-person team by sharing a staggered rotation of two weeks on and one week off, so that one teacher from the previous week would always be present in the next week's pairing. Although I don't advocate scheduling congregational worship and children's programs at the same hour, in those regions where this is the norm, parents should look for creative staffing arrangements that provide for both children's needs for stability and continuity and adult preferences for worship participation.

Some congregations use a combination of short-term volunteers and long-term adult spiritual companions. The Workshop Rotation model of religious education (a popular learning center's approach to children's programming) is designed to use workshop leaders who commit just three to five weeks of time and energy and a group leader (a "shepherd") who stays with a class of children for the entire program year as a facilitator and guide. The Godly Play model and its variations rely on a long-term worship leader who functions as the storyteller and principal teacher, along with multiple short-term volunteers who serve as assistant teachers (called "greeters") or manage logistical details (such as snacks). If a congregational program using one of these models has relinquished the long-term commitment requirement of the shepherd or storyteller roles, it will be difficult for children to establish close personal relationships with the adults who work with them and thus to see these adults as committed and trustworthy companions on a challenging and life-changing spiritual journey.

Nurturing relationships between adults and children can also occur outside formal religious education settings. Congregations wishing to foster children's spirituality provide opportunities for children and adults to spend time together and talk with one another about life, faith, and God. Such interactions may happen over coffee, juice, and cookies during the reception or fellowship time after congregational worship. They may occur on a congregational work day while children and adults are raking leaves or cleaning out cupboards together. They may emerge as part of the shared experience of painting walls at a local homeless shelter during a service project. My youngest son developed a close relationship with a sometimes cantankerous but warmhearted seventy-year-old deacon in one of my churches, as the latter taught him how to use a push broom to sweep the floor of the meeting hall each week after our postservice refreshment time. The children in another church swapped stories about what they had learned in church school while a normally staid and conservative elder taught them how to shimmy barefoot up the poles of that hall. I've witnessed a college-aged young woman painting children's nails and chatting about their daily lives and prayer concerns while providing child-care services for the adult choir. Some of these exchanges will occur spontaneously because of the personalities of the adults and children involved, but a congregation committed to nurturing adult-child spiritual relationships actively creates and encourages intergenerational interactions.

Attention to the Culture of Their Tradition

Because one of the main reasons for a family to affiliate with a congregation is to expand children's exposure to the language and practices of their faith tradition, parents need to find a religious

Other Adult Relationships as Childhood Assets

One of the findings of the Search Institute study described in Chapter One is that close relationships with adults other than their parents have a positive effect on children's lives. Listed as an external form of support, the study, published in *What Kids Need to Succeed,* describes this asset this way:

> Kids know other adults besides their parents they can turn to for advice and support. They have frequent, in-depth conversations with them. Ideally, three or more adults play this role in their lives.

> One way it suggests that congregations can contribute to the presence of this asset in children's lives is through the development of mentoring programs and intergenerational events that provide opportunities for children and adults to talk about their spiritual experiences and questions.

community that richly embraces the words, symbols, rituals, and rhythms of spiritual life within that tradition. One of the problematic trends of the last decade among religious institutions has been the movement away from clearly delineated identities in particular traditions to a more generic version of religious life that seeks more to avoid offense than to provide a framework for transformational religious expression. In the rush to discard problematic (and sometimes deserved) reputations as rigid, doctrinaire, and out of touch with reality, many faith communities no longer celebrate their "family ties" with a particular history nor value the rituals and language of their forebears. In the rush to mimic the formats and presentation of popular public events and places—rock concerts, movies, coffee houses, nursery schools—some congregations no longer provide an alternative reality to the messages and practices of mainstream social culture.

Such a congregation can do little to foster the type of biculturalism necessary to support children's engagement in an inward and outward spiritual journey that resists oppressive cultural messages and embraces life-giving habits and values.

Adults and children need religious communities full of signs that point toward God. They need communal rhythms that remind them of God's time and draw them into attentive listening to God's story of love and justice. Visual cues, like changing seasonal colors and familiar religious symbols, prompt us to remember how God has acted in the past and wonder how God might act today. The repetition of key words builds a vocabulary for talking about what these actions mean and how we can participate in them. Worship rituals that blend old and new forms of spiritual expression draw contemporary families into association with the long line of spiritual family members who have gone before them, much the way preparing great-grandmother's famous green-bean casserole or great-uncle John's holiday punch roots holiday celebrations in beloved family legacies. Ancient words of blessing reinforce the sense of God's unending grace; coupled with sermon illustrations drawn from the immediate experiences of contemporary lives, they help us see how God remains near to God's people throughout time.

Children and youth are fascinated by the similarities between their faith journey and those of people who lived long before them. When they dismiss adults (and their ancestors) as potentially irrelevant to how they construct meaning for their lives, it is because they don't want the experiences of "dead people" to be the final word in what they rightly understand is an ongoing process of spiritual connection with God. In a video production workshop I led a few years ago, a group of high school students eagerly set out to research how several biblical characters had lived the faith "24/7/365." With no prompting from me other than the names of several minor characters, references to where their stories could be found in the Bible, and a set of five open-ended research questions to help them explore the characters' lives, these young people voluntarily spent an hour poring over Bibles, dictionaries, maps, commentaries, and other resources looking for clues to how and why their characters lived faithfully.

Religious Culture Checklist

Every congregation creates a space in which
to gather and chooses words and images to define that space.
Use this checklist to help you determine whether a faith community is attentive to the symbols and language of its tradition in ways that will help your family develop a rich religious
identity for the expression of your spiritual experiences. If you
do not see or hear many of the items on this list, the congregation may not be able to adequately support the kind of spiritual enculturation you seek for your children.

- Visible symbols of the tradition (a cross, a scroll, a lamb, a cup,
  a rod) in conspicuous places
- Songs and hymns from a variety of time periods in the history
  of the tradition
- Preaching and teaching examples that draw on the stories of
  the tradition as well as the experiences of contemporary life
- Copies of the tradition's sacred texts visible and in use
- Symbolic colors in use and special furnishings in prominent
  view
- Words for important religious themes used as a matter of routine (and periodically explained in more familiar terminology)
- Depictions of faith stories on walls or in stained glass or other
  art forms
- Plaques or other items commemorating past members and
  ready explanations for the roles these persons played in the
  congregation

They invested another hour and a half comparing notes, deciding
what their key findings were, and producing a video titled "Heaven
Today," in which their characters appear in chronological order with
a heavenly talk show host who interviews them about their spiritual
life. The video closes with an improvisational version of the rock song

"I Will Survive," indicative of their conclusion that faithfulness throughout the ages is about standing up for what you believe in, even in the face of great opposition. Such powerfully formative ideas require opportunities to discover the wisdom of the past and its continued relevance for contemporary lives. Parents should look for congregations that appreciate the power residing in the language, symbols, and stories of the past and make them accessible to children as part of the religious culture of the community.

Characterized by Attitudes of Thanksgiving and Hope

The fifth mark of a congregation capable of caring well for children's spiritual formation is a communal attitude of thanksgiving for children's gifts and hopefulness about the role of children in helping to change the world. Faith communities sometimes delight more in the pleasure of holding babies or watching children engage in cute behavior than in the many other contributions children can make to the life and mission of a congregation. Children may also be celebrated more for their symbolic value as signs of future survival than as present-day contributors to a common spiritual life. But a congregation that sees children as good aspects of God's creation and vital parts of the body of faithful people looks for ways to encourage children to become the "history makers" of Walter Brueggemann's story-linking approach (as discussed in Chapter Three) to nurturing children's spirituality.

History-making is about becoming the story of faith through one's own attitudes and actions, such that others are moved to embrace God and the spiritual journey as well. Congregations facilitate this history-making process when they provide opportunities for children to express and respond to God's love through service to others. These service opportunities may take the form of internal service, such as providing compassionate care for weak or infirm members of the religious community or assisting with specific congregational activities. They should also involve acts of compassion, mercy, and justice with persons outside the congregation: with neighbors in need

Gauging Opportunities for Service

Ways to determine what opportunities you and your children will have to serve in and through a congregation include reading through the congregation's newsletters and checking out bulletin-board displays. Do published requests for help indicate that children are invited? Do the pictures of past projects include children? Are children among those thanked for their contributions? Can you imagine your child involved in the kind of activities described? If the answers to these questions aren't obvious from what you can read or see posted, ask church leaders or other parents whether children are generally included in service and outreach projects. If they say no, ask if they are open to the idea. Just because they haven't done it before doesn't mean they won't try it, if you're willing to lead the way!

and strangers who live nearby or far away. Children ought to be invited to help assemble flood response kits during hurricane season or school kits for children in underdeveloped countries. They need us to welcome them in the work of collecting blankets for the homeless and delivering them on a cold winter evening to those shivering on grates downtown. They should find among their spiritual family encouragement to canvas their schoolmates and extended families for clothing and shoes to contribute to a congregational drive. If their religious community limits its spiritual journey outward to checks written to unseen organizations or "adult-only" activities for the benefit of the poor and needy, children have to work harder at maintaining an appropriate balance of inward and outward spiritual responsiveness, and parents bear a greater burden of responsibility for nurturing this important integrative aspect of children's spiritual lives. Better that the entire faith community embrace the gifts and role of children in working to elicit a more just and loving world.

Never Give Up

The search for a congregational partner in the task of nurturing and sustaining our children's spiritual lives can seem a bit daunting to parents unaccustomed to probing the values and commitments of religious communities. Although the process may be similar to the hunt for a good day-care facility or excellent school district, the questions we must ask challenge us to keep reaffirming spiritual commitments and values that may not be widely understood and embraced by the faith communities we approach. Congregations have many ideas about what it means to be the people of God in the twenty-first century, just as schools have diverse ideas about how and what children need to learn in order to be competent thinkers and productive citizens someday. As parents, we may feel like novices trying to evaluate the experts without a full understanding of our subject of inquiry.

It may be helpful to think of the quest to find a faith community as a process of "trying on" life in various communities to see how well their practices resonate with the commitments we've embraced as part of our familial spiritual journey. Some practices may look different from our own and yet be consistent with our commitments. The language may contain different accents and inflections and still be derived from the same root tongue. Not all the criteria for being a strong nurturing community may be met at equally high levels, but we may see some degree of commitment or openness and be able to imagine how we can encourage more. Approach the process of finding a faith community to call your own as a tour through unknown but fascinating lands, remaining open to pleasant surprises, prepared for a bit of culture shock, and realistic about inevitable disappointments. Use the same care and high standards you would apply when selecting a caregiver or a weekday school for your child. Look for a congregation with enough light to enhance the spiritual flame you have lit in your family and that will expect you to contribute your glow to them as well. In such a place, you and your children will find companions for a life sustained in loving relationship with God and neighbor. You will no longer mutter, like the people of Maya Angelou's poem, hunting for the lost dimension of life. Instead, you will journey together within the dimension of divine love.

Helping Congregations Support Families

If you are already part of a congregation, you can help your congregation become a better place of nurture and sustenance for familial spiritual journeys. Invite a group of interested parents and church leaders to meet and discuss how they would answer the questions parents are encouraged to pose throughout this chapter. Do your answers correspond to the values and commitments expressed in this book? Are there some areas in which you need to improve your openness and commitment to children? How many items on the "Religious Culture Checklist" can you mark as present in your building and activities? Imagine you are a family visiting your congregation for the first time. As an adult, how do you know you are welcome? As a child, what are the signs that the people in this congregation were expecting someone like you and are glad you have come? As your group works through these exercises, look back at earlier chapters if you need specific ideas for improving your support for children's spiritual formation. The ideas that work well in the home work well in congregations, too!

THINKING ABOUT CHILDREN AND FAITH

QUESTIONS FOR REFLECTION AND DISCUSSION

Pausing after each chapter to think about how the ideas in this book relate to your own experiences, desires, and evolving perspectives makes us more fully partners in this conversation. If you share your reflections with a group of other adults who care about children, then the potential for collaboration expands even further, because now the conversation includes many more ideas, dreams, and experiences from which to draw inspiration and encouragement. It is in this spirit that I invite you to use the following questions. The language of each is directed to parents, but removing the personal pronouns would render them suitable for religious educators and other adults who work with children who are not their own.

Each chapter also contains sidebars, several of which pose questions or suggest activities. I have not repeated those materials here, so you might wish to review them for additional reflection and discussion ideas.

INTRODUCTION

1. Maya Angelou's poem suggests that a quest for love is a spiritual issue for many people. What has been the nature of your

own spiritual journey thus far? Illustrate your journey by drawing a timeline that shows significant spiritual moments in your life. What do you desire for your own spiritual life in the coming years? List your hopes for the future on the right side of the same sheet.

2. What are the concerns that motivate you to care about your child's spiritual life?

3. What are your hopes for your children and their spiritual lives? What are the dreams you harbor for them?

CHAPTER ONE

1. How have you heard the term *faith* defined in the past? How is that definition affirmed or challenged by the idea that faith is a gift from God rather than a set of beliefs? Do you think of yourself and your children as people who have faith?

2. In what ways have you experienced God's presence in your life? Describe a metaphor or image that expresses this sense of being connected to the divine.

3. In what ways do you see evidence of some of the age-related aspects of faithfulness present in your child? Which aspects seem absent at this time?

4. This chapter discusses six concepts (belonging, thanksgiving, giftedness, hospitality, understanding, and hope) that are important to faithful living. Which of these concepts are already significant factors in your children's lives? Are there other concepts you would include?

CHAPTER TWO

1. What kind of environment have you been trying to create for your child? What are the primary characteristics you want your child's world to have?

2. Who are the significant characters in your child's "neighbor-

hood"? What stories and imaginary worlds are important to him or her?

3. What values and assumptions are your children picking up from their environment? How are these ideas related to the values you would like them to have?

4. What do you think about the idea that children need to be raised with both a social world and a religious world? In what ways are your children already bicultural in the sense of having exposure to or affiliation with a religious community?

5. Think about what your family does during December. Are there ways in which your family's celebration of Christmas is already bicultural? How might you further emphasize the religious celebration of this holiday season?

6. Take a tour of your own home, either by walking through your house or reviewing each room in your mind. How are you creating an everyday spiritual world for your child to inhabit? What signs of your religious tradition are present? What toys do you already have that might encourage religious imaginary play?

CHAPTER THREE

1. How have your children been "receiving the story" of God's love and care for them? Make a list of the "camels" (the needs or baggage) your children bring with them that sometimes make caring for them more of a chore than a labor of love. What are some other ways you might welcome your children as they are?

2. Who might play the role of godparent in your child's life? Which children in your world might you godparent so that they have another link to their spiritual tradition?

3. When and how do your children "hear" the story of their spiritual tradition as well as their own stories? What books do you have in your home library to share, and to help you share, these stories with them?

THINKING ABOUT CHILDREN AND FAITH

4. What has your child done lately that you could celebrate as an act of charity and compassion? What did or might you do to recognize this linking of their personal story with their faith story?
5. Who in your family or community of faith encourages your children to "tell" their spiritual story in their own words?
6. In what ways is your child already a history-maker? How might you be history-makers together?

CHAPTER FOUR

1. Many people have Christmas carols, songs, or stories that they have known so long they can't remember exactly when they learned them. What songs and stories do you remember most strongly from your early childhood? Why do you think these are such vibrant memories? Are any of these memories about religious songs or stories? Why or why not?
2. Make a list of the religious words that your children hear over and over. Where do they overhear these words? When have you heard your children use these words for themselves?
3. Does your family know any communal prayers? When do you say these prayers together or with other people? In what ways do you think these prayers help your children to recognize that they are part of a larger spiritual community?
4. Which of the four guiding principles (clarity, richness, concreteness, and critical awareness) of religious language poses the greatest challenge for you? Which seems to be most challenging for your community of faith?

CHAPTER FIVE

1. Draw a line on a sheet of paper and label one end "quiet" and the other "noisy." Put a mark to illustrate where a typical day in your life falls on this continuum, remembering to consider

THINKING ABOUT CHILDREN AND FAITH

the quality of your interior life as well as the literal sounds around you. Place additional marks for each member of your family. Based on these marks, how familiar is your family with silence?

2. What might your children gain by practicing silence? How might your life be enriched by practicing silence with them, as well as on your own?

3. Which forms of prayer described in this chapter are most attractive to you as an adult? What is appealing about them? Which forms do you resist, and why?

4. Which forms of prayer can you imagine trying with your child? Which forms do you think would be more difficult to practice together? What makes some forms more attractive options and others less so? If you have tried some of these forms with your children, reflect on what may have surprised you about those experiences.

5. Think about the level of whining and complaining in your household. How might a family practice of lament change how you and your children deal with challenges, frustrations, and disappointments?

CHAPTER SIX

1. What is your concept of God? Where did your ideas about God come from (personal study, religious upbringing, familial teaching, a reaction to other perspectives, somewhere else)?

2. What seems to be your child's operative concept of God? Are there aspects of this concept that specifically please or concern you? Is there a particular way that you would like your child to view God?

3. What kinds of questions do your children ask about God and the spiritual life? How comfortable are you with their questions? What resources (including printed materials and other people) would you like to have around you as you encourage your children to engage in spiritual reflection?

THINKING ABOUT CHILDREN AND FAITH

4. How is your intuitive or bodily knowledge of the spiritual life the same as or different from what you think about spirituality? How do your children exhibit signs of different types of knowledge about being spiritual people? What religious rituals or body movements have you and your children learned?

CHAPTER SEVEN

1. Draw a "Journey Inward–Journey Outward" grid. Make your own list of characteristics for each of the boxes, or borrow those from the chapter. Where would you put yourself in the grid? Where would you put your child? Your religious community? Why?
2. Continue looking at your grid. If you placed yourself or your child in a positive square, what kinds of spiritual practices might help you dwell in that space well? If you or your child are in a negative square, what practices might help you move into the diagonal positive space?
3. In what ways do you and your children already participate in the spiritual "journey outward"? Which of these activities are primarily acts of compassion, and which are means of seeking justice? Are you more comfortable encouraging your children in one or the other of these types of activities?
4. Pick up a copy of your local newspaper or a national news magazine. What current news stories or events might lend themselves to "praying the news" with your child?
5. Who are the "crazy friends" who might support your family as you act out your spirituality together? Who are the adults around you who might welcome your children's participation in social outreach?

CONCLUSION

1. If you grew up in a religious community, how well did it meet the criteria for hospitality to children described in this chapter?

THINKING ABOUT CHILDREN AND FAITH

What did you appreciate as a child? What do you wish had been different?

2. If you are not part of a community of faith now, what concerns do you have about joining such a community? What excites you about the possibility?

3. If you are already part of a religious community, how well does it support you in your work of nurturing your children's spiritual lives? What changes could it make to become more supportive?

4. What are your child's assumptions about communities of faith? Are they, like Sam, reluctant to go to church, or are they enthusiastic about the idea? What do you think has influenced their perspective?

REFERENCES

❧✦❧

INTRODUCTION

See Maya Angelou's *The Complete Collected Poems of Maya Angelou* (New York: Random House, 1994); the passage is found on p. 228.

Read more of Anne Lamott's thoughts on the role of religious communities in children's spiritual lives in her book *Traveling Mercies: Some Thoughts on Faith* (New York: Pantheon Books, 1999), p. 100.

For those interested in exploring J. H. Westerhoff's classic question further, *Will Our Children Have Faith?* rev. ed. (Harrisburg, Penn.: Morehouse Publishing, 2000) is a good short introduction to contemporary concerns about children's faith formation.

CHAPTER ONE

P. L. Benson and others' *What Kids Need to Succeed* (Minneapolis: Free Spirit Publishing, 1998) provides a summary of the Search Institute study and suggestions for how parents, schools, communities, and congregations can cultivate assets in young people.

See Francis Gemme, translator, *The Confessions of Saint Augustine* (New York: Airmont Publishing Company, 1969), p. 143.

See Harold J. Grimm, ed., *Christian Liberty by Martin Luther* (Philadelphia: Fortress Press, 1957), pp. 39–40.

Chapter Two

For those interested in a more thorough explanation of acculturation theory, read Jean Phinney's "Ethnic Identity and Acculturation" in Kevin Chun and others' *Acculturation: Advances in Theory, Measurement, and Applied Research* (Washington, D.C.: American Psychological Association, 2003) or one of the other fine essays in this volume.

Find even more ideas in Phyllis Vos Wezeman and Jude Fournier's *Celebrating Seasons* (Mystic, Conn.: Twenty-Third Publications, 2000).

Debbie Trafton O'Neal's *Before and After Christmas: Activities and Ideas for Advent and Epiphany* (Minneapolis: Augsburg Fortress, 1991) provides an idea a day for the month before Christmas and several days afterward.

Explore James Kasperson and Marina Lachecki's *These Twelve Days: A Family Guide to After-Christmas Celebrations* (Cleveland: United Church Press, 1999)as part of your holiday celebrations this year.

See Erik Erikson's *Identity: Youth and Crisis* (New York: Norton, 1968).

Chapter Three

Walter Brueggemann's *Belonging and Growing in the Christian Community* (Atlanta: General Assembly Mission Board, Presbyterian Church in the United States, 1979) can be hard to find now that it is out of print. Check a local Presbyterian church library if you would like to explore his ideas further. His description of the five aspects is found on pp. 31–32.

See Anne Streaty Wimberly's *Soul Stories: African American Christian Education* (Nashville: Abingdon, 1994). Wimberly is in the process of revising this book; the second edition will focus specifically on story-linking for youth and families.

See Erik Erikson's *Childhood and Society* (New York: W. W. Norton, 1963).

These and more ideas can be found in Elaine Ramshaw's *The Godparent Book* (Chicago: Liturgy Training Publications, 1993), pp. 1, 10–11.

For those interested in a traditional story from a non-Christian tradition, see Dharma Publishing USA's *The Rabbit Who Overcame Fear* (Oakland, Calif.: Dharma Press, 1991). There are more than twenty storybooks in the Jataka Tales series.

Children of many ages love Marc Gellman's *Does God Have a Big Toe? Stories about Stories in the Bible* (New York: HarperCollins, 1989). Gellman's other book of midrashim is *God's Mailbox: More Stories about Stories in the Bible* (New York: Beech Tree Books, 1996). With Thomas Hartman, he has published *Where Does God Live? Questions and Answers for Parents and Children* (Liguori, Mo.: Triumph Books, 1991), and *How Do You Spell God? Answers to the Big Questions From Around the World* (New York: Beech Tree Books, 1995).

Enjoy Sandy Eisenberg Sasso's *A Prayer for the Earth: The Story of Naamah, Noah's Wife* (Woodstock, Vt.: Jewish Lights Publishing, 1996) with preschool or younger elementary age children. Sasso has a second book for older elementary and middle school children that I would classify as midrash: *But God Remembered: Stories of Women from Creation to the Promised Land* (Jewish Lights, 1995). Among the books she has written that link biblical stories or principles with contemporary life are *God in Between* (Jewish Lights, 1998) and *God's Paintbrush* (Jewish Lights, 1992).

Savor all the stories in Avril Rowlands's, *Tales from the Ark* (Oxford: Lion Publishing, 1993). Rowlands has also published *More Tales from the Ark* (Oxford: Lion, 1995), *The Christmas Sheep and Other Stories* (Intercourse, Penn.: Good Books, 2001), *The Animals' Easter* (Colorado Springs, Colo.: Chariot Victor Publishing, 2000), and *Rainbow's End and Other Tales from the Ark* (Oxford: Lion, 2002).

My children couldn't stop laughing over Martha Whitmore Hickman's *And God Created Squash: How the World Began* (Morton Grove, Ill.: Albert Whitman and Company, 1993).

Tomie dePaola has written or illustrated over a hundred children's books, many of them with religious themes. Books that illustrate the linkage of a human story and the biblical story are *The Clown of God* and the *Strega Nona* stories, as well as his story for children about the death of a grandparent, *Nana Upstairs, Nana Downstairs.*

The contrasting illustrations of past and present times are the best part of Peter Graystone and Jacqui Thomas's *If I Had lived in Jesus' Time* (Nashville: Abingdon, 1995), pp. 3, 8–9.

Judy Blume's *Are You There God? It's Me, Margaret* (New York: Dell Publishing, 1970) is an excellent glimpse inside the spiritual reflections of young adolescent girls. The quotation from Margaret's journal is on p. 61.

The African American characters in Patricia Polacco's *Chicken Sunday* (New York: Scholastic, 1992) are heartwarming and inspirational.

A young friend with leukemia found Jan Karon's *Miss Fannie's Hat* (Minneapolis: Augsburg, 1998) especially meaningful.

Even my graduate students find Marjorie Barker's *Magical Hands* (New York: Simon & Schuster, 1989) a moving spiritual tale.

The fact that Cynthia Rylant's *An Angel for Solomon Singer* (New York: Orchard Books, 1992) is set in our home state increases its value for my children. Ask your local librarian about spiritually uplifting books with some connection to your area.

Ralph Milton's *The Family Story Bible* (Louisville: Westminster John Knox, 1996) makes a good baby gift for families who want to begin reading Bible stories to their little ones from birth.

See Charles Sheldon's *In His Steps* (Uhrichsville, Ohio: Barbour Publishing, 1948).

CHAPTER FOUR

See what other similarities you can find between Dr. Seuss's classic, *Green Eggs and Ham* (Danbury, Conn.: Grolier, 1989) and the psalms and prayers your family is familiar with.

Find other ideas in Harold Bogot's piece "Making God Accessible: A Parenting Program" in *Religious Education,* 1988, *83,* 510–517.

Selina Hastings's *The Children's Illustrated Bible* (New York: Dorling Kindersley, 1994) and *The Illustrated Jewish Bible for Children* (New York: Dorling Kindersley, 1997) intrigue children from preschool through adolescence. Dorling Kindersley also publishes shorter collections of biblical stories, such as *The Miracles of Jesus* and a *Who's Who in the Bible* reference book using the same format.

The stories in Rahel Musleah and Rabbi Michael Klayman's *Shared Blessings: Children's Stories for Exploring the Spirit of the Jewish Holidays* (Woodstock, Vt.: Jewish Lights, 1997) encourage children to see themselves in the families portrayed.

Judyth Groner and Madeline Wikler's *All About Yom Kippur* and *All About Rosh Hashanah* (Rockville, Md.: Kar-Ben Copies, 1997) are small and light enough to tuck in a child's backpack. Kar-Ben also publishes holiday books by other authors.

Try out some of the great activities in Fiona Walton's *Let's Explore inside the Bible* (Minneapolis: Augsburg, 1994).

See *The Access Bible* (New York: Oxford University Press, 1999). The publisher provides an online resource with supplemental materials to support individual and group study.

Explore *The Learning Bible* (New York: American Bible Society, 2000). This Bible and reference book is available in print or on CD-ROM. The electronic version provides additional resource materials, including several scripture-based songs.

A wonderful collection, Mary Batchelor's *Children's Prayers From Around the World* (Minneapolis: Augsburg Fortress, 1995) is a great place to find special prayers to share during family celebrations.

See Barnabas and Anabel Kindersley's, *Celebrations!* (New York: Dorling Kindersley, 1997). This book and others in the "Children Like Me" series are available wherever UNICEF (the United Nations Children's Fund) products are sold.

For those more interested in Craig Dykstra's work, see *Growing in the Life of Faith* (Louisville: Geneva Press, 1999), pp. 125–126.

CHAPTER FIVE

Discover how to engage both heart and mind in prayer in Roberta Bondi's *To Pray and to Love: Conversations on Prayer with the Early Church* (Minneapolis: Augsburg Fortress, 1991), p. 10.

There are bound to be poems that engage the imagination of almost any child in Shel Silverstein's *Where the Sidewalk Ends* (New York: Harper & Row, 1974) and *Falling Up!* (New York: Harper-Collins, 1996).

Discover your own favorites in Maya Angelou's *The Complete Collected Poems of Maya Angelou* (New York: Random House, 1994); "Tears" is on p. 16.

R. S. Thomas is a Welsh poet and priest whose work reflects his deep struggle with and passion for the religious life. His *Mass for Hard Times* (Glasgow: Bloodaxe Books, 1992) invites the reader to wrestle with the ambiguities of life and religious practice, from the spiritual implications of cloning to the shape of congregational worship.

Mark Jarman is a poet and English professor at Vanderbilt University. My own favorite book of his poetry is *Questions for Ecclesiastes* (Brownsville, Ore.: Storyline Press, 1997), which contains twenty "Unholy Sonnets" exploring the human relationship with God as well as other poems.

A favorite poet with musicians and others who love music is James Weldon Johnson's *Complete Poems* (New York: Penguin Classics, 2000), edited by Sondra Wilson.

Explore Erika Langmuir's *Heaven in Art* (London: MQ Publications, Ltd., 1998).

See Karen Stone's *Image and Spirit: Finding Meaning in Visual Art* (Minneapolis: Augsburg, 2003), p. 157. Stone has a list of "101 Questions to Ask of an Artwork" that parents might use themselves or with their children if praying with art becomes a practice the family wants to cultivate.

In addition to the brief description of this special kind of prayerful singing on p. vi,

Taizé: Songs for Prayer (Chicago: G.I.A. Publications, 1998) contains words and accompaniment for several easy-to-learn songs.

See "Wesley's Directions for Singing" in *The United Methodist Hymnal* (1989). And while you're there, look for a favorite hymn or two for your family to sing together.

Enjoy Sandy Sasso's *God's Paintbrush* (Woodstock, Vt.: Jewish Lights, 1992).

See Ralph Milton's *The Family Story Bible* (Louisville: Westminster John Knox, 1996), pp. 116–117.

A beautiful set of recordings of Hildegard of Bingen's music has been made by the German women's group, Sinfonye, with members of the Oxford Girl's Choir. Released by Celestial Harmonies (www.harmonies.com), it is "The Complete Hildegard von Bingen, Volumes One and Two" (1999).

Henri Nouwen reflects on vocation and leadership in a short (eighty-page) volume titled *In the Name of Jesus* (New York: Crossroad, 1999).

Elizabeth Cady Stanton, a women's rights advocate and participant in the first Women's Rights Convention in Seneca Falls, New York, in 1848, edited *The Woman's Bible,* a commentary on the Old and New Testaments in light of a concern for women's equality with men. *The Woman's Bible* first appeared in print in 1898 and was reprinted by the Seattle Coalition on Women and Religion in 1974.

Jarena Lee was a nineteenth-century African American woman who understood herself to be called as a preacher in an era when neither women nor blacks were generally recognized in that role. Her autobiographical account of her story, "The Life and Religious Experience of Jarena Lee, A Coloured Lady, Giving an Account of her Call to Preach the Gospel. Revised and Corrected from the Original Manuscript, Written by Herself," was first published in 1836. It is included in a book edited by William Andrews titled *Sisters of the Spirit: Three Black Women's Autobiographies of the Nineteenth Century* (Bloomington: Indiana University Press, 1986).

Martin Luther King Jr.'s understanding of the relationship between the spiritual life and the fight for civil rights is well articulated in his book *Strength to Love* (Philadelphia: Fortress, 1963), which is a collection of fifteen sermons on faith, human rights, and politics.

To learn more about the spiritual struggle to make sense of suffering, read Harold Kushner's *When Bad Things Happen to Good People* (New York: Schocken Books, 1981).

See Lois Rock's, *A First Look: Prayer* (Oxford: Lion Publishing, 1996).

CHAPTER SIX

Audrey and Don Wood's *The Little Mouse, The Red Ripe Strawberry, and The Big Hungry Bear* (Singapore: Child's Play International) was first published in 1990, with the most recent reprint in 2001. Its companion book is *Merry Christmas, Big Hungry Bear* (New York: Blue Sky Press, 2002).

Karl Rahner's reflections on children's spirituality are discussed in David Hay and others' "Thinking About Childhood Spirituality: Review of Research and Current Directions" in Leslie Francis and others' (eds.), *Research in Religious Education* (Macon, Ga.: Smyth & Helwys Publishing, 1996.)

Further discussion of the study of "irreversibility" and other aspects of cognitive development in children can be found in Jean Piaget's *Six Psychological Studies* (New York: Random House, 1967).

Explore the many conversations John M. Hull had with his children in his book *God-Talk with Young Children* (Philadelphia: Trinity Press International, 1991).

See Harold Kushner's *When Children Ask About God* (New York: Schocken Books, 1976), p. 11.

There are several good ideas for families in Edith Bajema's *A Family Affair: Worshipping God with Our Children* (Grand Rapids, Mich.: CRC Publications, 1994).

Elizabeth Caldwell's ideas in *Making a Home for Faith: Nurturing the Spiritual Life of Your Children* (Cleveland: United Church Press, 2000) will give you plenty of options for beginning your own family practices.

See the Youth and Family Institute's *Faith Talk with Children* (Minneapolis: Youth and Family Institute, 1998).

More like a picture book than a text by a noted scholar, Robert Coles's (comp.) *In God's House: Children's Drawings* (Grand Rapids, Mich.: Eerdmans, 1996) is simple and spiritually thought-provoking for children and adults.

See Helen Oppenheimer's *Helping Children Find God: A Book for Parents, Teachers and Clergy* (Harrisburg, Penn.: Morehouse, 1995).

The Way Into . . . series includes, among other topics, "how-to" guides for praying, studying Torah, and exploring Jewish mysticism. The fourteen-volume set, published by Jewish Lights, is being developed over a three-year period, and each book is roughly 150 pages long.

See Arthur Green's *These Are the Words: A Vocabulary of Jewish Spiritual Life* (Woodstock, Vt.: Jewish Lights, 2001). Lawrence Kushner has a similar book titled *The Book of Words: Talking Spiritual Life, Living Spiritual Life* (New York: Random House, 1998).

The caricatures of God in Ralph Milton's *God for Beginners* (Canada: Northstone, 1996), pp. 61–66, are hilarious and telling.

Joan Chittister's book, *Illuminated Life: Monastic Wisdom for Seekers of Light* (Maryknoll, N.Y.: Orbis, 2000), is an abecedary in which the author takes twenty-six words (one for each letter of the alphabet) related to spirituality and provides meditations on the meaning of each term for the reader's devotional use. Chittister combines her meditations with a companion saying from the collections attributed to the desert fathers and mothers of fourth-century Christianity. The quotation is from p. 21.

CHAPTER SEVEN

I am indebted to Roy Oswald and Robert Friedrich Jr. and their book *Discerning Your Congregation's Future: A Strategic and Spiritual Approach* (New York: Alban, 1996) for the general conception of the Journey Inward–Journey Outward grid. Oswald and Friedrich have created several such grids for use in congregational planning; I have adapted their idea to reflect the structure and rhythm of personal spiritual lives.

Most of the stories and observations included in this chapter come from my work on the Faith Formation in Children's Ministries Project—a three-year study of American mainstream Protestant congregations and their ministries with children from birth to twelve years.

See Robert Coles's *The Moral Intelligence of Children: How to Raise a Moral Child* (New York: Penguin Putnam, 1997), p. 7. The

Augustine quotation is referenced on the page preceding the book's preface.

The Web site of the Carmelites of Indianapolis, www.praythe-news.com, includes not only information about the order's practices but links to several news sites and commentaries by the sisters on news stories that have moved them to prayer.

There are hundreds of ideas in Jolene Roehlkepartain's *Teaching Kids to Care & Share* (Nashville: Abingdon, 2000). The ideas represented (from pp. 16, 18–19, and 22–23) are, in some cases, slight adaptations of Roehlkepartain's descriptions so that the activities can be done by individual families as well as faith communities.

To learn more about the courageous families of Billings, Montana, read Janice Cohn's *The Christmas Menorahs: How a Town Fought Hate* (Morton Grove, Ill.: Albert Whitman & Company, 1995). Her other stories mentioned in this chapter come from *Raising Compassionate, Courageous Children in a Violent World* (Atlanta: Longstreet Press, 1996), which includes several stories of children (or children now grown up) whose compassion or desires for justice led them to lives of unusual service. A brief section titled "The Littlest Campaigner" highlights my older son's work on the Massie campaign.

For a classic book on families and social justice, you will find nothing better than Kathleen and James McGinnis's *Parenting for Peace and Justice* (Maryknoll, N.Y.: Orbis Books, 1981), pp. 93–108. Kathleen and Barbara Oehlberg are also the authors of *Starting Out Right: Nurturing Young Children as Peacemakers* (Oak Park, Ill.: Meyer-Stone Books, 1988).

See Jan Johnson's *Growing Compassionate Kids: Helping Kids See Beyond Their Backyard* (Nashville: Upper Room Books, 2001), pp. 142–143.

Conclusion

There is no end to the wisdom in Anne Lamott's *Traveling Mercies: Some Thoughts on Faith* (New York: Pantheon Books, 1999).

See Janet Marshall Eibner and Susan Graham Walker's, *God,*

Kids, & Us: The Growing Edge of Ministry with Children and the People Who Care for Them (Harrisburg, Penn.: Morehouse Publishing, 1996), p. 31. This is an especially good book for congregational leaders who want to nurture children's spiritual lives more fully.

See Peter Benson, Judy Galbraith, and Pamela Espeland's *What Kids Need to Succeed: Proven, Practical Ways to Raise Good Kids* (Minneapolis: Free Spirit Publishing, 1998), pp. 36–38.

THE AUTHOR

❧❖❧

Karen Marie Yust teaches Christian education and spiritual formation at Christian Theological Seminary in Indianapolis. A graduate of Harvard University with a doctorate in theology, she is also the mother of three children and an ordained minister, with dual standing in the United Church of Christ and the Christian Church (Disciples of Christ).

Previous publications include a theological guidebook for the media literacy curriculum, *Kids Talk TV: Inside/Out,* a post-9/11 article in *Disciple* magazine, "Mommy, Were Children on Those Planes?", an article on toddler spiritual formation in the *International Journal of Children's Spirituality,* and a handbook for congregations, *Attentive to God: Spirituality in the Church Committee.*

Yust served for eleven years as a parish pastor and conducts workshops on children and spirituality around the country. She is an active participant and presenter in the annual meetings of the International Conference on Children's Spirituality, which brings her into conversation with scholars, teachers, and religious leaders from all over the world. Her children help keep her humble by jokingly referring to her as "the Rev. Dr. Mom."

INDEX

Silverstein, S., 100
Social justice, 153–157
Solomon (King), 106–107
Songs, spiritual, for children, 76–77
Soul Stories (Wimberly), 42
Spiritual awareness. bodily knowledge and, 139–142; developmental sensitivity and, 124–127; intuition and, 139–142; reflective processes and, 123; teenagers and, 134–135; through artistic reflections, 133–134
Spiritual life, two aspects of, xxiii–xxiv, 144–150
Stanton, E. C., 109
Stone, K., 102
Stories, of faith tradition, 23–28, 73–75
Story-linking, and nurturing children's spirituality, 42–67
Story-living, 66–67
Storybooks, types of, 49–60
Storytelling, religious, xxv, 41–67
Study groups, for religious language acquisition, 79–81
Supplication, prayer of, 115–116
Swanson, J. A., 35
Synagogue. *See* Faith community

T
Taizé worship movement, 103
Tales from the Ark (Rowlands), 53
Teaching Kids to Care & Share (Roehlkepartain), 154–155
Teenagers: concepts of God and, 125; peer pressure and, 158–160; spiritual awareness and, 134–135; and value of service contributions, 160–161
Telling the story, and story-linking, 64–66
Thanksgiving, 15–16, 19, 117
Theodidacti (persons taught by God), 5
These Are the Words: A Vocabulary of Jewish Spiritual Life (Green), 136
These Twelve Days (Kasperson and Lachecki), 34
Thomas, J., 54–55

Thomas, R. S., 101
Toddlers: cultural values and, 26–27; developmental sensitivity and, 124–126; faithfulness and, 11–12, 14; religious language acquisition and, 75; sacred scriptures and, 129
Tower of Babel narrative, 51–52
Toys, for religious imagination, 36–38
Transformation, 10, 66–67
Traveling Mercies (Lamott), xxi–xxii

U
Understanding, and faithfulness, 17, 19

V
Veggie Tales (videos), 49–50, 64

W
Walker, S., 169
Walton, F., 78
Warhol, A., 101
Wesley, J., 104
Westerhoff, J., xxiv
Wezeman, P. V., 34
What Kids Need to Succeed (Search Institute), 173
"What would Jesus do?" items, 66
Where Does God Live? (Gellman and Hartman), 55–56
Where the Sidewalk Ends (Silverstein), 100
Wimberly, A., 42
Workshop Rotation, and religious education, 171
Worldviews, of children, 22
Worry, prayer and, 115–116
Worship services, and children, 166–170
"WWJD" items, 66

Y
Yom Kippur, 33
Youth and Family Institute, 131–133

Z
Zakat (almsgiving), 33, 151

CREDITS